Seeing Things

Seeing Things

◆ ◆ ◆

Television in the Age of Uncertainty

John Ellis

I.B.Tauris *Publishers*
LONDON ● NEW YORK

Published in 2000 by I.B.Tauris & Co Ltd
Victoria House, Bloomsbury Square, London WC1B 4DZ
175 Fifth Avenue, New York NY 10010
Website: http://www.ibtauris.com

In the United States and Canada distributed by St. Martin's Press
175 Fifth Avenue, New York NY 10010

ISBN 1-86064-125-3 (hardback)
ISBN 1-86064-489-9 (paperback)

A full CIP record for this book is available from the British Library
A full CIP record for this book is available from the Library of Congress

Library of Congress catalog card: available

Typeset in Garamond by A. & D. Worthington, Newmarket
Printed and bound in Great Britain by WBC Ltd, Bridgend

CONTENTS

Acknowledgement

Stills from the title sequence of *The Day Today* series one are reproduced with kind permission of the following: series production company Talkback Productions; Jump Graphics; Armando Iannucci (producer); Chris Morris (co-producer).

CHAPTER 1

INTRODUCTION

The television industry enters the new millennium in a state of profound uncertainty. Changes are taking place on all fronts. New production technologies are altering the ways that programmes are made; new distribution technologies are altering the experience of television viewing itself.[1] Ask senior managers for their prediction of how the medium will look in five years and they will simply shrug their shoulders and say they have no idea. This book is the product of trying to come to terms with this uncertainty, both as a producer and as an academic. When I began to write it, it had the working title of 'Television Doesn't Matter Any More'. Seeing the gentle decline in hours viewed and the promise of ever more channels, it seemed to me that the medium would no longer play the unobtrusively central role that it now has in everyday life. But, in trying to understand this role, I have become convinced that television will continue to play an important part in society, commensurate with the amount of time people spend in its company.

I try to place television in two different contexts. First, I examine it as one of the technologies of the audio-visual which have introduced a new modality of perception into the world, that of witness. Photography, cinema and television have confronted us with much more about the wider world than previous generations had encountered. They have done so through a particular form of representation that brings with it a sense of powerless knowledge and complicity with what we see. The essence of this sense of witness is that 'we cannot say that we do not know'. Television has brought this sense into the home, and intensified it with its pervasive sense of liveness and intimacy.

At the same time, television has participated in the development of post-war consumer society. Television as a key component of consumer society has already passed through two distinct eras. The first era of scarcity coincided with and promoted a period of standardized mass market consumerism. This was the phase of the development of public service broadcasting. The second era, that of availability, coincides with a much more diverse consumer market, which accentuates and commodifies every available difference between citizens in the name of choice. Television in the era of availability has taken on a new form, which I explore in some detail. In the era of scarcity, television tended to present definitive programming to a mass audience. Now it presents a diffuse and extensive process of working through. This takes the form of a constant worrying over issues and emotions, dealing with the feelings of witness through the presentation of a riot of ways of understanding the world without ever coming to any final conclusions. This open process of working through takes place across the great genres of television, and is significantly helped by the new graphic nature of electronic image processing. It is an accidental development rather than a planned one. But planning exists at the centre of television in the era of availability in the practice of scheduling. This little studied but crucial aspect of broadcast management is central in determining the nature of any television service and any national televisual universe.

Television's development from the era of scarcity to that of availability was a difficult one. I played a small part in the process in Britain, as one of the many independent producers contributing to Channel 4, which has done much to bring this new era into being in Britain. But Channel 4 has its own difficulties in this new era. These difficulties spring from its very founding principles which were developed in the era of scarcity. I examine Channel 4's problems as a product of a period of transition in Chapter 10. Leading on from this, I examine the possible shape of the emerging third era of television, the era of plenty, and in particular what the future role of generalist public service broadcasters might be in that new era.

All of this is an attempt to understand the nature of the medium that I have both worked in and studied for nearly twenty years. As such, this account is offered in the spirit of approach that Ien Ang has proposed:

> It is clear that the initiatives of the transnational media industries are bringing about significant and confusing transformations in the multi-

contextual conditions of audience practices and experiences. At the same time, these large-scale structural developments have made the predicaments of postmodern audiencehood ever more complex, indeterminate and difficult to assess, not least because of the [ubiquity] of these developments. There no longer is a position outside, as it were, from which we can have a total, transcending overview of all that's happening. Our minimal task, in such a world, is to explicate that world, make sense of it using our scholarly competencies to tell stories about the social and cultural implications of living in such a world. Such stories cannot be comprehensive, but they can at least make us comprehend some of the peculiarities of that world; they should, in the listing of Geertz 'analyse, explain, disconcert, celebrate, edify, excuse, astonish, subvert'.[2]

I cannot claim to have done all of those things that Ang specifies in drawing on Geertz's list, but I have offered a series of stories, of ways of coming to terms with television and the sheer size of television as a phenomenon. I have not tried to imply, as Ang might seem to, that there is some overall plan nurtured at the heart of the 'transnational media industries'. My feeling is, as is evident from my opening remark, that the whole process is rather more blind and arbitrary. This is a general point that I hope that I have made in relation to the development of the contemporary consumer economy as well. Such developments are the product of many forces, including that of chance: the patterns of cause and effect can be made out once they have happened, but the process itself is uncertain. And the feeling of uncertainty that haunts the modern world is one that I think that television addresses in an important and distinctive way.

That is another story, another way of making sense of what surrounds us. One of the products of the process of witness is that any contemporary citizen in the developed or developing world will have had access to far more pieces of information than can possibly be crammed into any explanatory framework. So there will be, I hope, those who can show the blindnesses and inconsistencies of the stories that I offer (including that of 'witness' itself). For the same reason, I do not claim to be making any blanket claim for all television as a socially useful or effective medium. However, much of what I have written concerns the more mundane aspects of broadcasting, the genres like talk shows, leisure programmes or documentaries that are often overlooked. Many criticisms of television reject the medium because of its relentless everyday ordinariness. I try to present this as one of television's founding strengths, which future developments will, if anything, intensify.

It is one thing to try to account for how television works, and a second to judge whether it is working well or badly in all or any of its particular instances. The stories that I provide offer the grounds for making discriminations, and though particular judgements are made, I do not mean to imply that television is of itself either necessarily good or bad. Though this might make for a good polemic, more subtle discriminations are required. Commentators jump too quickly to blanket condemnations of the medium, often based on quite justifiable objections to particular programmes or tendencies. But the nature of the medium itself is examined too infrequently, and scarcely at all through involving a historical perspective. If invited to provide a soundbite answer to the question 'Is television good or bad?' I would have to say simply 'It is both'. Its particular instances (whether broadcasting systems, channels or individual programmes) can be good or bad or indifferent according to the multiple decisions which frame them. Television itself occupies an important and changing role in modern society, and that is what we have to try to understand through the stories that are at our disposal.

This book has been a long time in the writing, and so there are many people whose contributions I must acknowledge.

First my partner Ros Coward who still, as I put it, watches programmes rather than television, and my children Carl and Harriet who have opened my eyes to many aspects of the medium through their enjoyment of it. My academic colleagues at Bournemouth University have provided much stimulation since I arrived among them; and my colleagues at the Institute of Media Studies at the University of Bergen have given me for many years now a valuable place to collect my thoughts and to test out ideas. The many producers with whom I have conversed over the years have, most of them unwittingly, provided me with important insights, and the contribution of those who have worked with me on many productions is inestimable. In particular I should thank the council members of PACT (the Producers' Alliance for Cinema and Television) and its predecessor body IPPA for deepening my professional involvement in the industry. Two events were important in clarifying the final draft of this book: a summer symposium at Ebeltoft in Denmark, organized by the University of Aarhus, and very soon after that a conference in Buenos Aires organized by the Antorchas Foundation. To single out individuals is invidious given how long this book has taken me to write, but I should mention three more. My editor Philippa Brewster, was the model of insistent patience, and provided detailed and perceptive comments when the manuscript was eventually delivered. Gavin Matthews checked and often researched the references, and Julian LeVay provided the title, which is usually the author's most difficult job.

---

[1] For two perspectives on these developments, see Brian Winston, *Media, Technology and Society: A History from the Telegraph to the Internet* (London: Routledge, 1998), and Manuel Castels, *The Information Age: Economy, Society and Culture* (Oxford: Basil Blackwell, 1996).

[2] Ien Ang, *Living Room Wars* (London: Routledge, 1996), p 79.

CHAPTER 2

WITNESS: A NEW WAY OF PERCEIVING THE WORLD

Culture and the Masses

We now live in a very crowded world. The globe has no true wildernesses any more: human activity has penetrated and affected everywhere from the remotest parts of Antarctica to the depths of the ocean. Natural resources are being depleted at an alarming rate. This is a new development in world history. Populations have grown exponentially since the end of the nineteenth century, and cities are growing fastest of all. Chinese business executives can now talk of the Pearl River delta as a supercity with an anticipated population of 100 million people. Since such populations are new in the history of the world, they require fundamentally different forms of communication in order to make an effective or even tolerable society.

Europe saw the first phase of such growth towards the end of the nineteenth century. Industrial society changed fundamentally as it entered the twentieth century and Europe's population grew enormously. Britain had 22 million citizens in 1851, and by 1911 this figure had almost doubled to 42 million. Thereafter the increase slowed so that the population in 1990 was stable at around 57 million people. This experience is reflected in most other nations of Europe, though, especially in some southern and eastern areas, the massive waves of emigration to the United States and South America delayed the growth in population totals. Europe's population growth slowed during the twentieth century, but that of the rest of the world did not. It took over a century for the world's population to grow from 1 billion (in 1805) to 2 billion (in 1926) but little over 30 years to put on another billion (1960), after which an exponential increase took place, with a population of 10 billion predicted for 2030.[1] The world became a mass culture in the twentieth century, and Europe and America led the way simply because the rapid expansion of population took place earlier there. So the development of many of the necessary forms of mass urban life originated in Europe and the USA, and, as is the case with cinema, this historical lead has conferred a continuing market domination.

The development of such large populations is not simply a quantitative change: it is qualitative. The nature of society and what individuals could do in it were fundamentally altered. With such numbers of people, society became overwhelmingly urban, more complex and subdivided. Simply to service the vast numbers of adults required many new forms of organization in the public infrastructure: of transportation, food supply and waste disposal, and communications. The processes of business and manufacture became more specialized and subdivided, creating new kinds of profession. The complexities of business towards the end of the nineteenth century vastly swelled the category of clerks, a kind of educated industrial proletariat, the 'white collar worker'. The forms of communication that would work for a city of a few thousand became hopelessly inappropriate for a city of over a million. Where a public meeting had been used as the means to communicate relatively effectively to the opinion leaders of the thousands, it was useless when faced by the new scale of population. So new forms of communication were developed, which produced a new area of economic activity and fresh possibilities for individuals. Newspapers required mass literacy, and mass literacy gave new possibilities for both work and leisure. The qualitative changes in society made possible changes in the lifestyle of many people living in the cities.

This is not to pretend that the process was an easy one. All changes have their losers as well as their winners; all changes destroy much that is valuable to many people. And this was especially so in Europe and the USA towards the end of the nineteenth century, when the pace of change and the ethics of those pushing it forward were such that scant attention was paid to its victims.[2]

Nevertheless, the standard of living of significant millions in the industrial cities was improving. A building boom took place at the end of the nineteenth century, whose marks can still be traced in the monumental late Victorian architecture still present in all the cities of Europe and America that were not destroyed by bombing. Large cities like London, Paris and Berlin, New York and Chicago developed suburbs which required sophisticated forms of mass transportation. Urban workers began to demand better and more diverse goods, well beyond the necessities of life. Consumer industries were beginning to develop, selling luxury goods for use in the homes of ordinary office workers and skilled industrial workers. Towards the end of the nineteenth century, homes began to acquire pianos, then gramophones and electricity. The growing need for office work had produced a literate class of clerks, eager to expand their knowledge through the consumption of books, magazines and newspapers.[3] All over Europe, the attractions of this urban life began to draw in many from rural areas, eager to escape the consequences of twenty years of agrarian depression, or the absolute poverty of a peasant existence.

Such were the conditions for the development of mass society. The term begins to be used – almost always in a pejorative sense – by intellectuals and moralists at the end of the nineteenth century. They did not like what they saw: newly confident 'ordinary people' with a little education, seeking a commercialized form of popular culture, and with money enough to enjoy themselves. Others, of course, had no such qualms, and set about providing whatever this new urban class required: music hall, popular opera, cinema, lurid magazines, sentimental novels, detective and Wild West stories. Then came cinema, providing, in its initial form at least, a means of entertainment that could break through the barriers of language and culture.[4] Governments were ambivalent about these developments; they enjoyed the tax revenues that accrued from this developing prosperity, yet worried, along with mainstream intellectuals, about the social consequences of the rather unruly entertainment that these new citizens seemed to favour. In Europe especially, broadcasting provided a solution that satisfied all parties when it developed during the 1920s with radio and then in the 1940s and 1950s with television. It provided the means by which entertainers and manufacturers could reach their audiences and potential markets, and at the same time it provided governments with a way to communicate directly with its citizens in their homes. It even, in the form of public service broadcasting, provided a medium through which intellectuals could try to educate the masses away from their 'low' culture to the 'high' culture enjoyed by intellectuals themselves. Yet cinema and broadcasting are not only a continuation of the development of a mass culture, though they of course share many of its characteristics. They brought something qualitatively different to each individual's experience of their society and the world beyond their immediate apprehension of it. They brought citizens into a relationship of direct encounter with images and sounds: a distinctive experience which I shall explore, the experience of witness.

The Century of Witness

The twentieth century has been the century of witness. As we emerge from that century, we can realize that a profound shift has taken place in the way that we perceive the world that exists beyond our immediate experience. We know more and have seen more of this century than the generations of any previous century knew or saw of theirs. The acceleration of communications has brought us word of so many events, so many peoples, so many places. We live in an era of information, and photography, film and television have brought us visual evidence. Their quasi-physical documentation of specific moments in specific places has brought us face to face with the great events, the banal happenings, the horrors and the incidental cruelties of our times. Perhaps we have seen too much. Certainly, 'I did not know' and 'I did not realize' are no longer open to us as a defence. We are all accomplices in the crimes, and the isolated successes, of the century. We are necessarily accomplices because we have seen the evidence and sometimes even the events themselves. We know about genocide; we know about the calculation of death in the millions. We know about famine and absolute poverty. We know because we have seen the images and heard the sounds which convey them. Equally we know the private lives of public people, politicians, stars and personalities. We know the insides of institutions that most of us will never visit: the gaols, the boardrooms, the homes of the great and of ordinary people whom we will never meet, the depths of the ocean and the peaks of mountains. We know them not as the abstract spaces of still photography but as living entities. We have been there. We have seen what goes on there.

If the images we have witnessed have not directly depicted events — some are too horrific, most take place beyond the gaze of the camera — then at the very least we have seen the evidence, the aftermath of distress and degradation. Images have brought the presence of these events to our attention in a very particular way. Photographic images bring us into the position of witnesses because they are mechanical reproductions. They have a relative inability to discriminate between subject and setting. Above all, they strike us with their haunting sense of being the death-mask imprint of a moment that is already past (if on film) or is fleeting and almost ungraspable (if on live television). Through the photographic image, we are drawn into the position of being witnesses ourselves to the events that took place in front of the camera. We are witnesses in another time and another space: we see the wars in the former Yugoslavia, genocide in Rwanda, the Vietnam War, Hiroshima and Belsen whilst we are in London, New York, Rio or Hong Kong. Very often, of course, we are witnesses not to the events themselves but to their immediate aftermaths. Like detectives, we are rushed to the scene of the crime hoping to make sense of what happened from the physical traces that it has left.

Photography, radio, and film all bring us into contact with this process of witness, but television has given it a purer definition because it makes an aesthetic promise that it is live, even though that promise is indifferently fulfilled. Each medium depends on a deep-seated cultural prioritization of the visual and the aural as the key means of apprehending and understanding the world. Each medium mimics our fundamental beliefs about what constitutes an adequate perception. Our language is shot through with the equivalence between the visual and the verifiable: 'seeing is believing', 'see for yourself', 'just have a look'. And equally, as George Bush memorably pointed out when he campaigned to become President of the United States, the conjunction of sound and image provides us with the key proof of sincerity. 'Read my lips: no new taxes,' he instructed the television audience. Once he was elected, new taxes became necessary nonetheless, and the repetition of the recording of his utterance with its evident sincerity was used effectively against him.[5] Moving images and sound depend for their effectiveness upon our attitude towards the visual and the aural: indeed, the push to develop them in the first place sprang from the same perspective.

Yet no-one would claim that to witness an event in all its audio-visual fullness is the same as being present at it. There is too much missing, both in sensory evidence (no smell, no tactile sense) and, more importantly, in social involvement. These lacks have so often been used to justify the argument that the audio-visual experience is a lesser experience than being present at an event. This is the conundrum of 'realism'. However, to treat the audio-visual as a form of witness is to realize that it offers a distinct, and new, modality of experience. The feeling of witness that comes with the audio-visual media is one of separation and powerlessness: the events unfold, like it or not. They unfold elsewhere and – especially in the case of film – another time as well. So for the viewer, powerlessness and safety come hand in hand, provoking a sense of guilt or disinterest. In another sense, of course, the act of witness is nevertheless powerful. It enables the viewer to overlook events, to see them from more points of view than are possible for someone physically present: to see from more angles, closer and further away, in slow and fast motion, repeated and refined. Yet at the same time, and by the very act of looking, individuals in the witnessing audience become accomplices in the events they see. Events on a screen make a mute appeal: 'You cannot say you did not know.'[6] The double negative captures the nature of the experience of witness. At once distanced and involving, it implies a necessary relationship with what is seen. The relationship is one of complicity, because if you know about an event, that knowledge implies a degree of consent to it. With this complicity comes an aching sense that something must be done. This in turn generates a new politics whose dimensions are only just beginning to emerge: a politics that says, as with the Kosovo conflict, that the world 'cannot stand idly by' in the words of Tony Blair. All of these consequences flow from a knowledge gained through a medium which mimics some of our direct sensory apprehension of the world.

The act of witness is never itself unmediated. Audiences have long been aware of the human mediation involved in the collection and dissemination of images. The films of Meliès, and Buster Keaton, *Hellzapoppin'* and many others reminded even the earliest of audiences that the most real-seeming media involve a degree of willing suspension of disbelief. Many commentators have treated such films as privileged moments, as exceptions in an aesthetic practice that otherwise was devoted to disguising the intervention of the human in the creation of moving images. Such critics, and I was one, thought it liberatory to advertise the constructed nature of images.[7] However true this might be, it was also a defence against the power that they have, the power which the idea of 'witness' tries to address. For however much it may be constructed, the photographic image does bring us into contact with individuals, crowds, actions and events, and this contact feels to a significant degree to be unmediated by other humans, however much they may have manipulated the footage. The reason lies in the fact that these are media of mechanical as well as human reproduction. As a result, photography and sound recording both provide a superabundance of information. There is always more detail than is needed by the narrative; always more present in the image than is picked out by the commentary; always more to be heard than the foregrounded sounds. We see the details of clothes and places, hear the distinctive and personal timbre of voices. Photographs have often been identified with a particularly wayward kind of attention, which seizes upon 'irrelevant' details, as Roland Barthes and Susan Sontag amongst others have noticed.[8] The effect can sometimes be jarring: a disaster victim weeps whilst wearing a Bart Simpson T-shirt. We choose to ignore the evident disparity and concentrate on their words; or we try to read a complex irony into this chance coincidence. More often, we can read the superabundance of details in any image or sound as the proof of its authenticity or the indicator of atmosphere. The recorded or live image and sound contain more than their manipulators, organizers and explainers can bring forward for our attention. Whether any viewing witness notices them is a matter for the vagaries of the individual viewing experience. What is important here is the fact that the sheer existence of this everyday superabundance of detail underpins the experience of witness. Witness is underwritten by the presence of the entirely unremarkable within the image, and of the 'atmosphere' of the sound.

If the image and sound were to contain only the information needed to make the point of the narration or to echo a written description of the events, then the sensation of witness would be virtually absent. Nevertheless, an unmediated event, if such were possible (or at least a minimally mediated event), would also fail to provide the sensation of witness. For the same superabundance of information would produce a sense of disorientation, not dissimilar to that experienced by contemporary viewers suddenly presented with some scenes from films made at the very beginnings of cinema. No action is foregrounded; everything is equally important and equally incidental. Television sport, from the first, felt the need for commentary for the same reason.[9] Simply to see is merely to sit before events. The sensation of witness demands a degree of direction of understanding. This level of narration is usually adequate for the viewer, and that is why the audio-visual media provide so much entertainment in our society. The sense of witness lies behind it, in the underlying superabundance of information contained within the images and sounds.

Realism

Witness is therefore a distinct category from that of 'realism'. Indeed, it avoids many of the confusions that are inherent in that much abused term. For the simple word realism contains a large number of muddled criteria.[10] Realism conflates questions of mechanical reproduction (as in 'the camera doesn't lie') with questions of the adequacy of the representation (as in '*Apocalypse Now* is more realistic than *The Green Berets*'), and questions of verisimilitude (as in 'Stephen Fry looks just like Oscar Wilde'). On the basis of such claims – which can often conflict with each other – realism quickly becomes an ethical category. The more a representation is deemed to be realistic, the greater its access to the truth of the situation. In the end, judgements about 'realism' come down to judgements about the relation between the object and its representation. And as, most of the time, knowledge of the object concerned is usually gained through the representation anyway, the argument becomes rather speculative. In any case, arguments about realism ignore what the many viewers of the representation bring to the experience. The reality of viewing is treated as a given. In writing about the cinema, the composition of audiences, the rituals of cinema-going, the apparatus of stars and entertainment and publicity, in short anything that frames and determines the viewing act, is simply ignored. When it comes to the examination of television, this becomes impossible, as television is consumed in so many different contexts and moods.

The sophisticated proponents of realism, like the French critic Andre Bazin, propose it as an impossible, though necessary, aesthetic aim.

> Realism in art can only proceed by way of artifice. Any aesthetic has to choose between what should be preserved, lost or rejected, but when that aesthetic claims to create the illusion of reality itself, as cinema does, then this choice constitutes its fundamental contradiction, one that is at once unacceptable and necessary. It is necessary because art can only exist through this choice. ... It is unacceptable because this choice is made at the expense of the reality that cinema proposes to represent fully.[11]

In a series of dense metaphors, he explores the processes of realistic depiction as a process of abstraction:

> In the usual way of making films ... the fact is attacked by the camera, cut into pieces, analysed and reconstituted; it does not lose its nature as fact for all this, but it is wrapped in abstraction like the clay of a brick is wrapped in the wall of which it will be a part, extending its dimensions.[12]

Bazin's accounts have the virtue of pointing out the impossibility of a mechanical reproduction of the sum total of experiences of any situation. However, his fundamental aim is a theological one. Much of his complex writing contrasts the outside appearance of an object or a situation with its inner essence or meaning. Bazin's realism depends on the distinction between accidents and essence, or, as it is commonly and so confusingly put, between 'appearance' and 'reality'. This distinction shows the extent of the conceptual collapses that can suddenly trap the unwary thinker who wanders into the realist edifice. In whatever sense the term is deployed, more often than not it is used to justify a subjective impression, or, as with Bazin, to smuggle in a particular theology by the back door. Lost under the weight of all this confusion is the fact of witness: a particular modality of the experience of recorded images and sounds, rather than an inherent quality to be found within those images. 'Witness' brings a model of the viewer's experience to the centre of the definition of the audio-visual without entangling it with ontological arguments about the relationship between representation and its objects.

Witness is a new form of experience; it arrived with the development of mechanical media which accord with how we believe we perceive everyday reality. So photography was the first medium to bring this particular kind of experience to the modern world; cinema, radio and television followed. Each medium promised more than it could provide, and each medium had specific economic and technological problems involved in its spread and full implementation. So the new perception of witness evolved gradually through the century. Only in the second half of the century did commentators begin to explore its specific nature which allows us to experience events at a distance, safe but also powerless, able to over-look but under-act.[13] And, further, we are now able to understand how witness brings us into a complicity with those events: 'We cannot say we did not know.'

---

[1] See Eric Hobsbawm, *Age of Extremes: The Short Twentieth Century 1914-1991* (London: Michael Joseph, 1994) and J.M. Roberts, *The Penguin History of Europe* (London: Penguin Books Ltd, 1995), pp 421, 472, 609.

[2] The process of the Industrial Revolution destroyed societies and individuals alike, through sudden action or by the long-term processes of ruthless exploitation of working people. This has left its traumatic mark in many ways: in the novels of writers like Charles Dickens, in the architecture of our cities, in the moving testimonies gathered by writers like Frederick Engels, in the politics of socialism, in the yearning for the countryside in the hearts of most of the urban population.

[3] See, for example, John Carey, *The Intellectuals and the Masses: Pride and Prejudice among the Literary Intelligentsia 1880-1939* (London: Faber and Faber, 1992).

[4] A comprehensive history of cinema is provided by: Benjamin Hampton, *History of the American Film Industry* (Mineola, NY: Dover Publications, 1970); Douglas Gomery, *Movie History: A Survey* (Belmont: Wadsworth, 1991); Geoffrey Nowell-Smith (ed), *The Oxford History of World Cinema* (Oxford: Oxford University Press, 1996); Kevin Brownlow, *The Parade's Gone By* (London: Secker & Warburg, 1968); and David Bordwell *et al.*, *The Classical Hollywood Cinema* (London: Routledge, 1988).

[5] Anders Johansen gives a brilliant demonstration of the effects of such displays of sincerity within the political process in his essay 'Credibility and Media Development' in Jostein Gripsrud (ed), *Television and Common Knowledge* (London: Routledge, 1999).

[6] A remark coined by Trevor McDonald, the Barbados-born anchor-man for many years of *News at Ten*, the main evening news on ITV, who was once voted the most trustworthy man on television. He utters this remark as a justification of the activity of television news in the documentary *40 Years of ITN* (produced by ITN in 1995).

[7] One of the main sources for approach was the *Screen* magazine debate on the Brechtian ideas of distanciation and separation, especially in *Screen* 16/4 (Winter 1975/6), the transcript of the 1975 Edinburgh Festival Brecht event.

[8] See Roland Barthes, *Camera Lucida, Reflection on Photography* (London: Cape, 1981); Susan Sontag, *On Photography* (London: Penguin, 1978).

[9] A brief history and analysis of the importance of commentary to television sport can be found in Gary Whannel, *Fields in Vision: Television Sport and Cultural Transformation* (London: Routledge, 1992), pp 26-32.

[10] A good source of further reading on this subject is John Corner, 'Presumption as theory: realism in television studies', *Screen* 33/1 (Spring 1992).

[11] 'Mais le réalisme en art ne saurait évidemment ne procéder que d'artifices. Toute esthétique choisit forcément entre ce qui vaut d'être sauvé, perdu ou refusé, mais quand elle se propose essentiellement, comme le fait le cinéma, de créer l'illusion du réel, ce choix constitue sa contradiction fondamentale à la fois inacceptable et nécessaire. Nécessaire puisque l'art n'existe que par ce choix. ... Inacceptable puisqu'il se fait en définitive aux dépens de cette réalité que le cinéma se propose de restituer intégralement.' André Bazin, *Qu'est-ce que le cinéma?*, vol 4 (Paris: Editions du Cerf, 1962), pp 21-2 [my translation].

[12] 'Dans le découpage cinématographique habituel ... le fait est attaqué par le caméra, morcelé, analysé, reconstitué; il ne perd sans doute pas tout de sa nature de fait, mais celle-ci est enrobée d'abstraction comme l'argile d'une brique par le mûr encore absent qui multipliera son parallélépipède.' *Ibid.*, p 32.

[13] Such as Laura Mulvey, *Visual and Other Pleasures* (Basingstoke: Macmillan, 1989). See also, Christian Metz, *Psychoanalysis and Cinema: The Imaginary Signifier*, trans C. Britton (London: Macmillan, 1982).

CHAPTER 3

WITNESS THROUGH THE TWENTIETH CENTURY

Photography and Witness

Photography irrupted into a world of print, in which the act of witnessing events was essentially a mediated one. Reporters gave written voice, more and less effectively, to what they had seen. Their reports explicitly involved selection and judgement, the creation of a narrative and the attribution of quotation. The best of them aspired to a personal voice. They stood between their audience and the events of the day. Photography was not so much a challenge to this approach as an adjunct. Weeks after the newspaper reports, it showed something of the logistical horrors of the Crimean War.[1] Photography's function of witness was limited to an 'I told you so' function by the cumbersome technological aspect of its early years. Later on, its distinctive contribution to our culture began to be fully realized. Photography's function of witness has opened up the world to our eyes in ways that written accounts of witnesses alone could never dream of achieving.

The use of photography began to change at the very end of the nineteenth century. Two developments were key: the introduction of moving cinema images, and the development of newsprint technologies that could reproduce photographs rather than steel engravings. Both emerged at the same moment and were put to rather different ends. Their early history is tangled and halting. It was not until the 1920s that 'photographic realism' became a term for writing that claimed to have purged itself of the subjectivity of its writer. This is an indication of how long it took to establish standard photographic and cinematic practices of witness. In the first years of the twentieth century the first dramatic shift was in the way that news came to its vast newly literate or barely literate audiences. Newspapers found that they were able to present their readers with photographs of events, rather than engravings. At the time, this seemed more like a useful technological advance than a fundamental change, but it inaugurated a substantively different attitude to perceptions of the wider world. Up to that point, news reporting had been a matter of heavily mediated accounts of eyewitness reporters. Print provided those accounts in writing, and an artist would render an impression of them in a steel engraving, sometimes made from memory of the event, more often derived from the imaginations incited by eyewitness accounts. What would seem huge infelicities and inconsistencies were commonplace, and they were accepted because engravings were held to render the essence of the event rather than its outward appearance. When newspaper photography arrived, the self-evident artefact of the engraving was replaced by something altogether more treacherous: the mechanical intervention of the camera. Observers at the time interpreted the change as a triumph for objectivity: the automatic eye of the camera was replacing the subjective eye of the artist.[2] Now, in retrospect, we can say that something rather different had happened. The photograph was bringing individuals into a different relationship with the world that lay beyond their immediate experience, the world that came to them as news. The consumer of news no longer had to rely upon delegating their involvement in the event to another individual, known at best simply by their by-line. The photograph carried with it a powerful charge of direct witness that the engraving and the written report did not.

Photographs could present a particular instant in a scene in its entirety. The camera does not select only the essentials, although those will normally be at the centre of the frame. The surrounding, unimportant or irrelevant details also appear, rendered with the same degree of faithfulness. This fact worked with the feeling of direct witness to give the consumers of the photographic image a sense that they were able to judge the events for themselves. The presentation of incidentals, things which might well be overlooked by an eye-witness reporter, were key to this process. Unmediated by any reporting voice, it seemed that the photograph provided a small degree of witness independent of the interpretive framework of reporters. Newspaper photographs of criminals allowed readers to indulge in their own psychological speculations about their character. Newspaper photographs of the 'scene of the crime' enabled readers to be their own Sherlock Holmes.

Cinema and Witness

At much the same time, cinema emerged from a thicket of nineteenth-century attempts to record and reproduce motion using photographic and other processes. To record and to reproduce were significantly different aims. Eadweard Muybridge made his famous series of photographs in a scientific attempt to analyse motion into its component parts. Motivated by the desire to reproduce motion, Reynaud created his Théâtre Optique which could display astonishing animated scenes.[3] Both tendencies, therefore, had known considerable achievements before the formal introduction of cinema to a paying audience. This fact has prompted reconsiderations of the received accounts of the introduction of cinema. These hold that cinema amazed its first viewers. But what were they amazed at? It was not so much that they saw vivid photography of everyday and exotic life. Lantern slide lectures had made that commonplace. Neither was it that they saw the subject of the image in motion, for ingenious showmen had achieved that with the magic lantern too, and in colour. The most astonishing thing was that everything in the picture moved, 'even the leaves on the trees' as one observer put it. It was the motion of the incidental details in the frame, rather than the essential subject, that so captivated those early audiences. It was the sudden ability to witness the incidentals of life just as they were that produced the effect of witness. No artist, and no moving parts in the lantern slide, could have rendered those details. Photography had the ability to capture everything that lay in front of the lens. The film camera was able to give it all motion. Together they introduced the audiences of a century ago to a new potential to witness events and phenomena in the world around them.

Yet even as cinema launched the experience of witness through its indiscriminate presentation of incidental motion, some observers experienced a sense of disappointment or even of loss. The Russian realist novelist Maxim Gorky, under a pseudonym, reported on his first experience of cinema at a fair in Nizhny Novgorod in 1896:

> Last night I was in the kingdom of shadows. If only you knew how strange it was to be there. It was a world without sound, without colour. Everything there – the earth, the trees, the people, the water and the air – is dipped in monotonous grey. … It is no life but its shadow, it is not motion but its soundless spectre.[4]

Gorky's experience was perhaps not unusual. Edison had tried from the beginning of his work with the cinema apparatus to marry sound reproduction with moving pictures; and experiments with colour photography, tinting, toning and frame-by-frame colour stencilling are a constant feature of cinema's early years. All these attempts to push the technology – many of which were successful and had a commercial life – betray the same vague sense of dissatisfaction with the cinema apparatus. For Gorky, it is clear, cinema promised more than he could possibly expect, yet at the same time provided less than he wanted. It allowed paying audiences to witness actions in an unparalleled way, certainly, but not as they happened. The startling presence of the events on the screen emphasises the viewer's separation from them, a separation that is both physical and temporal. This separation was experienced sometimes as a sense of loss, sometimes as a sense of inadequacy of the representation. But it is a defining characteristic of cinema, and so became the source of its enduring strength. Photography gives us presence at whose heart lies a sense of absence. Therein lies its particular emotional register, and its easy intimacy with the obscure workings of human desire.

Perhaps this is one of the reasons why factual cinema had such an unhappy history. The Lumière Brothers themselves were convinced that the phenomenon of cinematic witness would be a powerful but transient attraction.[5] They sent their camera teams to the end of the navigable world to show film and bring back footage of ever more

exotic places. It was an elegant piece of business. A Lumière techni-
cian, equipped with a combination camera-projector would travel to
a far-flung place (many were much more remote than Nizhny
Novgorod). He would set up and photograph street scenes that were
then projected back to local audiences along with images of other
places and even short comic gags. The footage of the place in
question was brought back to Paris and became another exotic image
for others in other remote places to witness, along with metropolitan
audiences. The Lumière Brothers were milking their invention
because they thought it would have a fashionable life of three or four
years. In one sense they were right. Cinema soon exhausted the
potential audience for the sheer act of looking, for simple witness
rather than witness of something. Events were needed, but the
technology was not well suited to capturing them. The machines of
photographic reproduction were cumbersome, expensive and limited
in their scope. No-one could afford to wait around for an interesting
event to take place. As an American cable station once memorably
put it, 'No-one knows when news will strike'.

As the showmen of the lantern-slide entertainment knew, fiction
film-making, creating events in front of the camera, was altogether
more practical. They became film-makers exploring the potential for
story-telling that lay within the new medium as well as satisfying the
abiding demand for witness of real events. Initially, this sensible and
effective solution was applied even to news events. Fiction films
were made showing imaginative interpretations of contemporary
events. Films of the Boer War offered what are to our eyes outrageous reconstructions of events that owe more to the staging of
popular melodramas than to anything happening in South Africa.
James Williamson's *Attack on a Chinese Mission* (1900) was famously
filmed at his own house in Hove, with a cast who looked anything
but Chinese.[6] What Williamson and the other film-makers were
offering was not an event to be witnessed by cinema audiences, but
an imaginative rendering of an already known event in exactly the
same spirit as the artists of newspaper and magazine. There are few
reports that anyone was disappointed by these films. The cinema was
invoking the convention of newspaper steel engravings, and adding
the sophistications of movement, parallel action and cross-cutting
between scenes. But it was doing so just at the same moment as
those engravings were losing their adequacy for their readership as
newspapers began to employ photography.

Confusion followed. Conventions for factual depiction proved very difficult to establish, at a time when fiction film-making was a riot of experiment. When Meliès explicitly advertised his painstakingly reconstructed version of the *Coronation of Edward VII* in 1902, made with official supervision, he was roundly condemned for fakery. Remembered too often as the founding master of cinema special effects, Meliès in fact had a far more complex project. His care in setting up the film of the coronation demonstrates a concern for correct detail. He consulted with the Palace staff and ecclesiastical authorities responsible for organizing the event, overcoming their instinctive suspicions. His intention was simple: since he was not allowed to photograph the actual events inside Westminster Abbey, he would provide an exact simulacrum of them. He found his Edward VII look-alike in the person of a Parisian butcher. (The real king, himself no stranger to turn-of-the-century Paris, is alleged to have been greatly amused by the exactness of the resemblance.) As an additional guarantee of his fidelity to the event, Meliès, as his publicity material attests, made it quite clear that his film was a reconstruction and not the real event. So, two years after Williamson's cavalier attitude to such questions, Meliès might seem to have been, if anything, over-scrupulous. Yet his film was met with condemnation for fakery, and the reception arguably cut short this new direction in his career.[7]

The difference of reception between Williamson's film of 1900 and Meliès' of 1902 shows that a significant shift was taking place. The photograph, still or moving, seemed to provide a superior form of witness: superior because unmediated. Cinema was showing that it could take the process of still news photography still further by animating those photographs into a simulacrum of the process of time passing rather than, as with the photography, of a moment snatched from it. Cinema had impressed the public with its ability to render in movement not only the core of events but also the incidentals. And now, with the increasing confidence and spread of film cameras, some real events began to appear on the screens. Film of the Siege of Sidney Street in January 1911 allowed people to see a shoot-out between police and anarchists on their own streets, and to compare what they witnessed on the screen with the accounts (written and photographic) that were printed in newspapers. Yet such footage remained a rarity. The cinema did not become a predominantly factual medium, to the great regret of the various reformers and improvers of mankind who had the vision to

appreciate its potential. The dream of direct witness through photographic reporting remained, exactly, a dream. For, as the First World
War was soon to prove, it could well turn out to be a nightmare.
Cinema's ability to bring audiences into a relationship of witness
with events made it possible to watch unbearable scenes of suffering
and disaster. It provided the promise of being able to witness real
executions, as indeed the first great film of Mexican cinema, *El
Automovil Gris* (1919), shows at its conclusion.[8] It provided the
possibility that ordinary citizens could see the disturbingly incomprehensible things that went on in the world. No government, and
even few entrepreneurs of the period, were prepared to allow this to
happen in anything but a very controlled way. So the First World
War saw the development of a rough protocol around the coverage
of events. Events could be staged in an accurate, but sanitized, way.
Almost a century later, we take those staged images as the reality of
the war.[9] It would have been possible to show the everyday gruesome realities of trench warfare (but not the sporadic set-piece 'over
the top' attacks), but no-one involved wanted to risk the probable
revulsion that would be felt by audiences at home. The First World
War was the first test of the censorship of the new aesthetic of
photographic witness, and it set a pattern for the future. A general
sense seems to have settled over the new medium that this new
aesthetic of witness was perhaps more terrifying than it was exciting.
During the period, the modernist poet T.S. Eliot coined the memorable dictum: 'Humankind cannot bear very much reality',[10] and for
the first half of the twentieth century this proved true. It took
another, even more terrible, world war to shake this belief.

Cinema increasingly developed away from exploiting its potential
to provide witness to the events of the world. As radio gave a sense
of instantaneity to news and to the transmission of human speech,
cinema newsreels of the 1930s took on a slightly ritualistic quality of
showing the people from whom the audience had already heard, and
events reports of which they had already read. Cinema stood in
much the same relation to news as the photographs of the Crimean
or American civil wars stood to the printed reports of them. There
was a distance of time involved which emphasised the distance of
space. In fact, the whole machinery of entertainment cinema developed this aspect of loss, absence and desire. The film stars, present
on the screen yet absent from the audience physically and tempo-
rally, became the focus for a sustained examination and experience
of the psychological and emotional dimensions of human relations.

Film-making retreated increasingly from any function of witness of public events in the same moment that it found that such a function was possible. Instead, it lavished its witnessing gaze on the physiology and psychology of stars, much to the wrath of those film-makers who believed in the almost God-given power of the cinema to provide a direct witness of everyday reality.[11] Cinema audiences of the 1920s, in the new and lavish picture palaces, saw the faces of the stars massively and in detail and learned to read them. The cinema was a wonder of physiognomy. Shakespeare once put it that 'there's no art to find the mind's construction in the face'.[12] Cinema provided a way of so doing.

But this was not simply an experience of witness: it was successful precisely because it exploited the sense of absence and the desire for presence that is the central characteristic of the cinema image. The cinema that developed to address a mass audience worked as a machinery of desire, in which audiences could invest their imaginations. It provided the means by which they could participate in different, better worlds, or exorcise their anger about the world they inhabited through the fantasies of crime fiction. There is always a lurking sense of absence at the heart of the fullness that is the cinematic spectacle. We know that the actors in any fiction are not performing in front of us at the same moment as we appreciate the astonishing illusion of their presence. Cinema used this, working on the evident disparity between the ordinary lives of the audience and the extraordinary lives of film stars, on and off the screen. Cinema's censorious critics never failed to point out this disparity. So loud has their criticism been, and so ingrained are the habits of thinking that divide reality from fantasy, that the real cultural place of cinema's achievement was not acknowledged for many years. If cinema deals in desire, in the absence that lies at the heart of its sense of presence, then the sheer difficulty of its project is awesome.

The more cinema developed as a means of mass entertainment, the more the absence of presence developed as a problem for it. This was particularly acute in the period between 1895 and the end of the 1920s, when technologies for the synchronization of sound and picture were not in widespread use. As Miriam Hansen described in *From Babel to Babylon*, cinema audiences remained a problem, especially in the cities. This was a time of mass immigration from Europe to America. 15 million people from all over Europe emigrated between 1899 and 1914, 'the greatest period of mass migration in recorded history',[13] and the majority went to the United

States. American cities were filling with people who brought different cultures and languages with them. Cinema audiences were
formed of individuals and small groupings, unknown to each other,
drawn from across these divides. They had to be brought together
into a collective mood that would allow a film to be watched in
sympathetic circumstances. For a long time, and even after films
began routinely to talk at the very end of the 1920s, live performances within the cinema were used to weld the audience together
into a collective experience of imagination and desire.[14] The images
on the screen could not (or were not) trusted to achieve this by
themselves. So the audience coalesced around stage entertainers,
talent shows, bingo games, sing-alongs, and many other traditional
live entertainments so that they could most easily and effectively
appreciate the performance of the film. Every film performance was
a risk, especially in the big picture palaces that were built all over
America and Europe, and in the big cities of the world as well,
during the 1920s. The scale of the image, its physical distance and its
sense of absence-in-presence all contributed to a problem of secur-
ing audience consent.

Looked at in another way, cinema's particular relationship to witness gave birth to that aching desire which haunts much of the
aesthetics of the twentieth century: the often frustrated desire for
(and fear of) an experience of direct witness. Photography promised
to provide it, yet the available technologies of photography were able
only at rare moments to fulfil this promise. The desire for full
photographic witness haunts the century as it develops. The potential for the experience of witness seemed to offer an objective form
of evidence, yet the technology that would provide it remained
hopelessly inadequate for the task. Cinema took the promise of
photography and added motion, introducing the twentieth century to
the possibility of a dramatic new sense of witness, but it could fulfil
that promise only fitfully. Both cinema's difficulties and its strengths
come from its special inadequacy in relation to a desire for witness
which it had itself stimulated, and which had called it into existence.
Cinema, as William Uricchio argues, was felt even when it arrived as
not enough: 'a look at broader cultural practices, at the telephone, at
ideas sparked by electricity, at fantasies of the new media, all suggest
that simultaneity stood as a powerful anticipation which film could
stimulate but never deliver. And there is reason to believe that film
audiences understood these limits.'[15] Photographic witness was
developing in one direction, but sound was discovering different

potentials. The telephone had already educated many people in the potential of live transmission of sound over spatial distance. What many expected from cinema was the same function for pictures: in other words, television. Developments in the field of sound, rather than the image, had conditioned this expectation.

Witness and Sound

Histories of cinema tend to treat sound as a late arrival to the party: unevenly present as an element of live performance during the so-called 'silent' era, and arriving in the form of synchronized dialogue at the end of the 1920s. Yet as many scholars have pointed out, this is a gross oversimplification.[16] Experiments with recorded and synchronized sound are as old as cinema itself, and during the early years, the major technological problem was one of finding an adequate form of sound reproduction that could fill a cinema hall.[17] More fundamentally, sound production had experienced a historical development of its own, one that is less recorded because it was more domestic. Before the introduction of viable public cinema shows, and before the mass reproduction of news photography, sound was being spread instantaneously from point to point, and could be reproduced using a highly convenient technology. The telephone had been introduced in 1877 and by the time cinema came along, more than a million phones were in use in American homes and businesses.[18] Significantly, too, telephone technology was used as a 'means of transmission of entertainment to groups of subscribers isolated in their own homes:

> The most popular feature of the Paris Exposition Internationale d'Électricité of 1881 was ... variously described as the theatrephone and the electrophone. ... In one, listeners heard live performances of the Opéra ... in the other they heard plays from the Théâtre Français. ... In Europe entertainment uses of the telephone were often an aristocratic prerogative ... [but] commercial interest in a larger, less exclusive audience was not far behind. 'Nickel in the slot' versions of the hookups provided by the Theatrophone Company of Paris to its individual subscribers were offered as a public novelty in some resorts. A franc brought five minutes of listening time, fifty centimes half as much. ... In England in 1889 a novel experiment permitted 'numbers of people'

at Hastings to hear *The Yeomen of the Guard* nightly. ... For the International Electrical Exhibition of 1892, musical perfomances were transmitted from London to Crystal Palace, and long-distance to Liverpool and Manchester.[19]

The gramophone virtually coincided with cinema in its commercial introduction, with the first spring-driven players becoming available in 1896.[20] Unlike cinema, both the telephone and the gramophone were consumer technologies, destined for everyday use in a domestic setting. They had, in this sense, more in common with the television than the cinema. And as cinema developed its vocation as medium of desire, a further domestic apparatus of sound was introduced: the radio. Its adoption was truly astonishing. In Britain the BBC developed a base of some 6 million licences to receive radio signals (in a nation of some 15 million households) in the ten years between 1922 and 1932, a figure which climbed again to 9 million in 1942.[21] Sound reproduction had a separate development to that of moving image reproduction and the element of absence, so crucial in cinema's development, was far less central. Telephony involved distance, but a live exchange of voices. Radio involved distance, but a live transmission of voices and sounds. The telephone call quickly became an established social fact. Indeed one of the standard tropes of the early cinema is 'the telephone call' from the victim to the potential rescuer (typically wife to husband), bridging space, yet emphasising physical distance that the rescuer has to cross.[22] The gramophone, far more than cinema, embodied Walter Benjamin's contention about mechanical reproduction: that it enabled the work of art to appear and perform itself in contexts wholly foreign to that of its first appearance, freed of any intention that might have surrounded its creation.[23] Yet it has taken until the closing years of the twentieth century for the implication of this development really to come to the attention of media historians. And the reason is simple enough. Since both technologies took their place in a domestic context, their social spread and effects took place beyond the reach of sociologists or social historians.

These technologies of sound readjusted attitudes to speech. Before, speech had been an irrecoverable, yet central, aspect of human activity. Records of speech were artificial and inadequate to the real texture of pronouncements. The standard written forms contained almost no information about hesitation, speed and tone of delivery or slips of the tongue. They rarely contained information about patterns of pronunciation or accent. This is the very materiality of human speech, to a significant degree its defining characteristic in interpersonal relations. The technologies of sound reproduction suddenly revealed this materiality to the population as a whole. Telephony's distant relay and the gramophone's wax recording gave the world startling new ways to witness speech. At the same time Freud was putting a great stress upon the importance of this materiality of speech in the understanding of character and motivation.[24] It is no accident that the term 'Freudian slip' was the first psychoanalytic insight to enter popular culture, and it is still the most widespread legacy of that pioneering work. Freud gave meaning to what people were witnessing for the first time as somehow having significance. Thanks to sound recording, the concrete utterances of individuals could be recalled, rather than mediated and inadequate accounts of them. Increasingly as the century continued, shrewd business people like Mary Pickford, the former film star, recorded their telephone conversations.[25] Increasingly, too, politicians were called to account for what they had actually said, rather than what they claimed to have said, as is still the convention with the accounts of British parliamentary debates in *Hansard*. By the Reagan era in the 1980s, the idea of 'mis-speaking' had to be invented to describe the frequent way in which the President came out with linguistic or policy gaffes, rather than what his entourage wanted him to say in the circumstances. Sound recording allows an act of witness to the utterance itself rather than to its record (if any) in the different medium of writing.

The development of sound recording in some ways parallels that of the cinema. The phonograph record was not exploited for the recording of speech so much as for music, as Michael Chanan so elegantly explores.[26] The ability to recall for subsequent witness a fleeting performance changed perceptions of music and the general appreciation of music during the twentieth century. It elevated the status of performance and reduced that of composition. Indeed, recording provided the conditions for performance-based popular music, from jazz, through 'crooning' to the modern popular music industry. Music became central to sound recording, and to radio transmission as well. However, radio was from the very beginning a broadcast medium using speech to cement its bond of live connection with the audience. But when cinema finally produced viable technologies of sound synchronization and reproduction, the film industry's leaders did not at first imagine that it would be used for speech.[27]

Sound and Cinema

Many of the first experiments with adding sound recording to cinematography were motivated by the desire to add a standardized music track to silent pictures. It was partly an economy measure, enabling theatre owners to do away with the need for expensive (and sometimes inadequate) live musicians. But it is also a sign of how important the regulation of the act of film performance had become, how difficult it was for some films to weld their patrons together into an audience. Consistent and high quality recorded music accompaniment seemed to be the answer. The addition of recorded speech seemed full of fresh problems, since film audiences in different regions and countries would have major problems of comprehension. Foreign markets, it seemed, would be lost if speech was added. The Warner Brothers initially intended the sound-track for *The Jazz Singer* in 1927 to consist simply of songs and music, but the marketing appeal of synchronized speech overruled their initial caution. Other more commercially successful experiments with sound were from the outset more attentive to the innovative features of radio broadcasting. William Fox concentrated on sound newsreel production, combining the live recording of sound and picture to capture such events as Charles Lindberg landing after his transatlantic flight as well as numerous entertainment acts. So the triumphant assertion of recorded speech by Al Jolson – that exuberant 'Wait a minute, wait a minute, you ain't heard nothing yet' in *The Jazz Singer* – came as a disappointment only to the cost-cutting Warner Brothers and their fellow moguls who saw the expense involved in producing multiple language versions.

When the recording of sound was married to the photographic act of witness at the end of the twentieth century's second decade, the century's profound shift in perception was well under way. Phonograph recording, though mainly limited to music, had thoroughly accustomed the industrialized world to the idea that fleeting sounds and performances could be retrieved from the onward flow of time to be heard again. The telephone had long since accustomed people to hearing known voices at a distance and radio had already grappled with the problem of hearing unknown ones, often with unfamiliar accents and unaccustomed vocabularies. So the cinema was inheriting a growing aesthetic of sound witness, which it grafted on to its central practice of the witnessing of psychological nuances.

The sound cinema began to engineer a closer relationship with audiences, and the practice of using live performances to make an audience coalesce very gradually fell away.

During the Second World War and its aftermath, cinema recovered something of its ability to provide witness of public and cataclysmic events. Again very little war footage exists that was real, and most of that has the curiously inconsequential feeling of mundane reality. John Huston's record of the battle for Monte Casino provides some of the few feet of actual battle that we have. As bullets fly past the camera (we are told), we see nothing of the drama of war, just a few trees and buildings. On the way to the front, however, we witness corpses and the hurried disposal of the bodies of American servicemen. Huston's film remained unreleased, with the United States War Department commenting dryly that it was not their business to release anti-war films.[28] For cinema audiences at the time, however, the war was depicted through judicious mixtures of accurate reconstructions and real events away from the front.[29] Cinema's devastating mobilization of direct witness came at the very end of the war. A whole generation was marked by seeing the footage from the concentration camps. This footage was not only generated by the liberating allies, filming what they found. It also, and horrifyingly, came from records of the SS themselves, recording their attempts to annihilate entire races of human beings. The act of witnessing this footage was hard to endure. It is clear that Alfred Hitchcock was probably unable to bear watching the hours of footage of the death camps that he was supposed to direct into a propaganda film at the end of the Second World War. After two weeks' work in July 1945, he returned to the United States, leaving the editor Stuart MacAllister to complete the film.[30] George Steiner's famous conundrum, 'Can culture be possible after the death camps?', can only be posed in the context of a culture which has forced itself to witness such events, and to witness them on a mass scale. Many saw this footage in the cinema. Billy Wilder, in an interview with Volker Schlondorff, recounted how, as head of the US Army's Psychological Warfare division in 1945, he forced German audiences to watch the footage by making it a condition of obtaining their bread rations. Others, including me, first saw the images reproduced in newspapers or in paperback books, as they were throughout the 1950s and early 1960s. An entire generation saw what humans were capable of doing to their fellows. By virtue of the mass circulation of these images alone, the post-war world would qualify for the designation 'the world of witness'. However, television also emerged during this period, and gave a definitive twist to the development of the century of witness.

Television: Live Witness Realized

Unlike cinema, television was consumed at home, just like radio's speech and sounds. Unlike cinema, television's images were live, as radio and telephony were. Of course, all kinds of qualifications immediately tumble in. Nothing in television's technology determined that it should be a domestic medium, for many early uses took place in cinemas or public halls, as the British film *Radio Parade of 1935* shows in its anticipation of television as a public spectacle. Television had the capacity to show filmed material from its very beginnings, and even in the early years of American broadcasting, many shows which appeared to be live were in fact filmed or at least recorded on film from a TV signal.[31] This stemmed from the basic nature of American television with its different time zones and system of quasi-autonomous local stations. However, the important fact is that all these programmes appeared to be live. The announcers talked directly to their audience; the singers sang directly to them; the comedians spoke to them as if from downstage, if not on an even more intimate person-to-person basis. Direct address, an exceptional and rarely successful event in cinema, was a commonplace of television. It produced the sensation that television was predominantly live, that the audience was hearing and seeing things as they happened. In the early years, this was indeed the case, for almost all the genres of television apart from news were live.

Television's sense of liveness does not depend solely upon its programmes; it also lies in the very organization of transmission. Transmission is live, even when the programmes are not. So recorded programmes are able to claim the status of liveness for themselves simply because the act of transmission attaches them to a particular moment. Broadcasting on television adopted and intensified the forms of radio broadcast, where a single transmission was beamed out from a particular place to a widely dispersed audience, who were all listening at the same moment. Broadcasting lived the same moment in time as its audience. Its audience, though fragmented, had the powerful sense that many others were listening at the same time. Television broadcasting brought images of one place to all those other places in the same instant. The separation and absence that characterized the cinema, and made it such a suitable vehicle for fiction, were not a necessary part of television; far from it. Television allowed its viewers to witness remote events as they happened. Television provided its audiences with a powerful sense of co-presence with the events it showed. It provided them with a sense of togetherness in separation with their fellow audience members. It reached its audiences in their homes. Television made the act of witness into an intimate and domestic act. It took away the sense of presence and absence which characterized cinema and replaced it with a sense of instantaneity.

Initially at least, the events that television audiences witnessed were limited to those which could easily be controlled, and those which were relatively easily accessible to the cumbersome technology that characterized its early years. It would be a long time before television wildlife programmes could show their audiences pictures of wild birds to match the sounds that were recorded for BBC radio nature programmes by Ludwig Koch in the late 1940s. Instead, viewers 'looked in' on peculiar spaces which were called studios, in imitation of the film industry (which itself had adopted the term to acquire a veneer of artistic respectability). Studios provided simulacra of places and events that television could not reach, as well as providing a neutral space for performers, particularly those adept at light entertainment in the direct address mode. At the same time, studios were used for a wide range of live drama productions of great ambition. Very soon, these simulacra developed their own particular intensity. Live television drama had a quality that contrasted strongly with that of the cinema, whose visual fluency it shared. It had the intensity of chamber drama, with sudden outbursts of emotion, and the uncertain rhythms of speech and action whose slight awkwardness gave them a naturalistic feeling when compared to contemporary cinema films.

Live television drama exists no longer, having been replaced by more filmic modes of mise-en-scene using rapid change of scene, real locations, complex spaces and movements. Those who regret its passing are mourning the first real development in our culture of the sense of live witness. The best of live television drama brought its viewers into extreme proximity with outpourings of emotion, or the visible marks of emotional repression. It was an experience unlike either the cinema or the theatre. It was unlike cinema because performers and viewers were held in the communion of a single moment, rather than being separated by time. It was unlike theatre because viewers and performers were not in the same space, and because viewers had a mobility of viewpoint, produced by the use of multiple cameras and the ability to give extreme close-up. Separated in space yet united in time, the co-presence of the television image was developing a distinctive form of witness. Witnessing became a domestic act, happening in the home rather than in a public space of entertainment. It came through a technology that proposed itself as a live transmission from a centre to millions of homes watching the same images at the same time. Television sealed the twentieth century's fate as the century of witness.

Live performance gave television a direct and intimate link with its audience, and this link became one of the defining characteristics of broadcast television. Nowadays, paradoxically, virtually no television is live apart from the news. Sport is the one genre that has maintained its status as live event: the best way to see a football match, a horse race or any other competitive event is as it happens, before the result is known. For all other kinds of output, from the simplest conversation to the most elaborate drama, the history of television genres is the history of the development away from live performance and transmission to the pre-recording of programmes that are then edited. However, with the exception of drama, television scarcely behaves like a pre-recorded medium. Programmes adopt the rhetoric of liveness without being literally live. Presenters still adopt the stance of direct address. Not only do they look directly into the camera and adopt a casual person-to-person form of speech, they also use all the indicators of co-presence. They talk of 'now' and 'today', 'here' and 'we'; they use the present tense. They use all those speech indicators whose meaning is context-dependent in order to orient themselves as speaking in the same moment of time as their audience hears them. Other indicators of co-presence include the repeated buttonholing of the viewer: 'Stay with us', 'Coming up', 'Soon', the indicators of a shared continuity of experience. All of this is a rhetoric, planned and learned, which enables a show to appear as live. The presence of a live audience (live, that is, at the point of recording) will help to ensure that the 'illusion of liveness' is maintained, of course. But the truly remarkable feature of this pervasive television practice is the willing participation of the viewer in this illusion. It is both pervasive and unnoticed, and, indeed, is necessary

for much television to be able to work with and relate to its audience. The illusion is so strong, and so much desired, that it can
function even when the programme patently is not live.

A clear example is *Blind Date*, a key early Saturday evening programme on ITV, presented by Cilla Black. The format is one of
those devastatingly simple light entertainment ideas that are very
difficult to execute in practice. Three candidates for a date are
presented. They sit behind a screen and are asked three questions by
the potential date, the 'picker' in the jargon of the show. A studio
audience and TV viewers can see both sides of the exchange. The
picker makes their choice, meets the two rejects and then their date;
together they choose a holiday destination and depart on their date.
The next week they return and tell what happened. This format
unrolls twice in each programme: 'boy' picks from 'girls'; the outcome of last week's boy's choice is shown; 'girl' picks from 'boys';
the outcome of last week's girl's choice is shown. The whole thing
takes place within a highly ritualized format (including in-jokes about
Cilla's residual Liverpudlian accent: 'huur' for 'hair' etc), and is
increasingly stuffed with innuendo. For several years, *Blind Date* has
been for many of the young and not-so-young British viewers the
early Saturday warm-up for the real-life sexual rituals of the later
evening. It has a sense of co-presence with its audience which is so
strong that it is able to present itself as live and be taken as a live
programme whilst its internal time-scale is clearly impossible. *Blind
Date* has a strong sense of irony – its ritualized exchanges are riddled
with a knowing archness – but in the matter of its sense of liveness,
no real irony is present. Indeed, it depends upon its illusion of
liveness for it to work at all for its audience.

Cilla bounds on and immediately sets up the programme's
chronology with a series of time-dependent utterances whose form
ranges from 'Welcome to tonight's *Blind Date*' to 'Later in the show
we will see how last week's contestants did'. And it is these 'last
week' segments that reveal the extent of the illusion of liveness. We
see a flashback to the revelation of the date; a short video of highlights of the holiday; the couple's introduction into the present tense
of the film; their pre-recorded comments on each other with their
present tense reactions vignetted in the bottom left of the screen;
then a present tense discussion with Cilla about what happened on
the date, a discussion whose explicit premise is 'Will they see each
other again?' and implicit premise is 'What did they really get up to
on the date?'. The whole chronology is a transparent fiction. The

events clearly happened in the order in which they are presented, but not in the claimed time-scale of a week. Within one week, this couple have met, gone on holiday for several nights, returned, recorded comments about each other, and appeared in the studio. This is clearly more than one week's activities. The distortion of time is intensified by the graphic demands of the pre-recorded comments sequence which superimposes the 'now' of the programme on those comments. In order to make the time gap clear, the participants at least wear different clothes, and sometimes have utterly different hairstyles. And just to render the whole process just that little more unbelievable, the holidays are often patently unseasonal. *Blind Date* is quite capable of claiming at the beginning of November that 'last week' a couple went to Poland and wore T-shirts surrounded by the lush greenery of midsummer.[32] And yet this fiction does not matter at all. The programme's internal time can be a total fabrication, one that could easily call in question the programme's claim to be happening 'now'. Yet it does not. *Blind Date* is a triumphant piece of popular entertainment, and the whole show depends for its connection with you the viewer, creating that sense of 'they're living what we're living'. This is why *Blind Date* deploys the rhetoric of liveness so effectively.

In our visually oriented culture, the co-presence that television provides is a powerful recompense for the loss of the other senses involved in physical witness: smell and touch. These senses provide the strength of our feelings of proximity, but the fact that we undervalue them is evident from the extent to which they lack a language in our culture. Television therefore pushed the development of its technologies to provide ever greater opportunities to witness in degrees of liveness and intimacy. This is particularly evident in news technology, where the push to provide ever more contemporary images began early and has reached the point at which wars and the noise of wars can be experienced in the home at the same time as on the battlefield. It sometimes seems that the only limitation placed upon this technology is that of military censorship, preventing the access of camera crews to the battlefield, or the reflexes of self-preservation in those camera crews themselves. Such is the culture of witness that we have developed. Or is it? For even news events are very rarely live; they only seem that way by their address to our sense of television's liveness. The reality of our witnessing culture is more complicated and nuanced. We desire the live-seemingness of news events and of the broadcast video image in

general. But this desire is mediated by a number of other factors: our
need for explanation and context; our sense of impotence in relation
to the events that we witness; and, nowadays, our growing sense of
the relative unimportance of television compared to the power we
once thought it had. Television has provided us with the suspicion
that unmediated live witness might be more of a threat than a
promise. As if in answer to this suspicion, television has developed
as an important means of dealing with the psychic problems of
witness, by developing a process which I will examine in Chapter 6
as one of working through. Television has made witness into an
everyday, intimate and commonplace act, as well as giving it a new
characteristic: that of liveness. Television has been able to develop in
this direction because of the nature of the consumer economies that
at once produced it and, to a significant degree, were also produced
by it. The process through which television embedded itself in
consumer culture and developed with it is the subject of the next
two chapters.

---

[1] For a study of early photography in war, with examples, see Gus Macdonald, *Camera: A Victorian Eyewitness* (London: BT Batsford Ltd, 1979), pp 79-90.

[2] See Eric Hobsbawm, *Age of Extremes: The Short Twentieth Century 1914-1991* (London: Michael Joseph, 1994), pp 192-3.

[3] For the career of Eadweard Muybridge, see Gordon Hendricks, *Eadweard Muybridge* (New York: Grossman, 1975) or Kevin MacDonnell, *Eadweard Muybridge* (Boston: Little Brown, 1972). For Emile Reynaud, the *Macmillan International Film Encyclopedia* (Ephraim Katz, London: HarperCollins, 1998, p 1153) has this to say: 'In 1888 [Reynaud] began painting his images directly on strips of perforated celluloid, approximately the width of the now-standard 35mm. From 1892 to 1900 these films were shown to huge audiences at the Paris Musée Grevin as an attraction called "Théâtre Optique".'

[4] Quoted in Jay Leyda, *Kino* (London: Allen & Unwin, 1983), p 23.

[5] For more information on this, see Alan Williams, 'The Lumière Organization and "Documentary Realism"' in John L. Fell (ed), *Film Before Griffith* (Berkeley: University of California Press, 1983), and Thomas Elsaesser, 'Louis Lumière: the cinema's first virtualist' in Thomas Elsaesser and Kay Hoffman (eds), *Cinema Futures: Cain, Abel or Cable?* (Amsterdam: Amsterdam University Press, 1998).

[6] See Frank Gray (ed), *The Hove Pioneers and the Arrival of Cinema* (Brighton: University of Brighton, 1996).

[7] Jacques Delandes and Jacques Richard, *Histoire comparée du cinéma*, vol 2 (Tournai: Editions Casterman, 1968) gives a detailed account, pp 453-63 including a long quotation from an anonymous newspaper article that they attribute to Meliès himself, though it is written in the third person: 'A French journalist wrote a truly grotesque article in Le Petit Bleu in which Meliès, after all his efforts to produce a serious and artistic work, is accused of being a common forger! This is what it cost

our inventor for having attempted, too soon, to make a "reconstruction" whilst audiences still believed that "if it is a photograph, then it must be true". This article obviously made him burst out laughing because no Englishman could have been taken in by the Ceremony In The Abbey because Warwick [the distributors] had widely advertised detailed explanations of the way in which the ceremony had been reconstructed.' Deslandes and Richard also reproduce Warwick's catalogue entry for the film and a detailed article from the *Daily Telegraph* of 20 June 1902 to support Meliès' claims for the film. I am indebted to Mme Malthete-Meliès for drawing this to my attention.

8 See John King, *Magical Reels: A History of Cinema in Latin America* (London: Verso, 1990), pp 19-20.

9 A fact deduced by careful examination of the footage by Roger Smithers of the Imperial War Museum's Archive. For a vivid demonstration of this, see the Channel 4 education series *The Reel Truth* directed in 1994 by Colin Thomas and produced by Teliesyn Ltd.

10 T.S. Eliot, 'Burnt Norton', *Four Quartets* (London: Faber & Faber, 1944).

11 The *locus classicus* is John Grierson's attacks on Hollywood in the early 1930s. Grierson wrote that 'The penalty of realism is that it is about reality and has to bother for ever not about being "beautiful" but about being right. ... Documentary was from the beginning ... an anti-aesthetic movement.' Forsyth Hardy (ed), *Grierson on Documentary* (London: Faber and Faber, 1979).

12 Macbeth, Act 1, Scene 4.

13 Hobsbawm: *Age of Extremes*, p 88.

14 See Miriam Hansen, *Babel and Babylon: Spectatorship in American Silent Film* (Cambridge: Harvard University Press, 1991).

15 William Uricchio, *Media, Simultaneity and Convergence: Culture and Technology in an Age of Intermediality*, text of Professorial Inaugural Lecture, Faculteit der Letteren, Utrecht 1997.

16 Such scholars include Kevin Brownlow, with *The Parade's Gone By* (London: Secker & Warburg, 1968) and Michael Chanan with *The Dream That Kicks: The Prehistory and Early Years of Cinema in Britain* (London: Routledge, 1982).

17 For the problems of sound, see Douglas Gomery, 'The coming of the talkies: invention, innovation and diffusion' in E. Weis and J. Belton (eds), *Film Sound* (New York: Columbia University Press, 1985).

18 Brian Winston, *Media, Technology and Society: A History from the Telegraph to the Internet* (London: Routledge, 1998), p 53.

19 Carolyn Marvin, *When Old Technologies Were New* (New York: Oxford University Press 1988), pp 209-10

20 Michael Chanan, *Repeated Takes: A Short History of Recording and its Effects on Music* (London: Verso, 1995), pp 28-9.

21 Asa Briggs, *The BBC: The First Fifty Years* (Oxford: Oxford University Press, 1985), p 166.

22 See, for instance, Tom Gunning, 'The Lonely Villa and the de Lorde tradition of the terrors of technology' in Annette Kuhn (ed), *Screen Histories* (Oxford: J. Stacey, 1998).

23 Walter Benjamin, 'The work of art in the age of mechanical reproduction' in Walter Benjamin (ed), *Illuminations* (London: Fontana, 1970).

[24] Sigmund Freud, *Jokes and their Relation to the Unconscious* (London: Routledge & Kegan Paul, 1966).

[25] The Mary Pickford Foundation in California holds these records.

[26] Chanan: *Repeated Takes.*

[27] See Gomery, 'The coming of the talkies'.

[28] See Midge Mackenzie, *Guardian*, G2 supplement, 23 October 1998.

[29] For further information see Anthony Aldgate and Jeffrey Richards, *Britain Can Take It: The British Cinema in the Second World War* (Oxford: Basil Blackwell, 1986).

[30] See Dai Vaughan, *Portrait of an Invisible Man* (London: British Film Institute, 1983), pp 154-5.

[31] For further information, see William Boddy, *Fifties Television: The Industry and its Critics* (Urbana: University of Illinois Press, 1990) or Christopher Anderson, *Hollywood Television: The Studio System in the Fifties* (Austin: University of Texas Press, 1994).

[32] This particular instance occurred on 1 November 1997.

CHAPTER 4

THE FIRST ERA OF TELEVISION: SCARCITY

Television's distinctive development of the sense of witness took place in the second half of the twentieth century, and already it is possible to distinguish three eras of that development. The first era is characterized by a few channels broadcasting for part of the day only. It was the era of scarcity, which lasted for most countries until the late 1970s or early 1980s. As broadcasting developed, the era of scarcity gradually gave way to an era of availability, where several channels broadcasting continuously jostled for attention, often with more competition in the shape of cable or satellite services. The third era, the era of plenty, is confidently predicted by the television industry itself. It is foreseen as an era in which television programmes (or, as they will be known, 'content' or 'product') will be accessible through a variety of technologies, the sum of which will give consumers the new phenomenon of 'television on demand' as well as 'interactive television'. The era of plenty is predicted even as most nations and individuals are still coming to terms with the transition to the era of availability.

A Modernizing Consumer Object

The era of scarcity was the era of television's introduction into society. It inaugurated the experience of witness as an everyday, large scale activity. It built upon radio's success as a live domestic medium to bring live pictures into the home. Television was able to do this because it was introduced at a particular point in the social and economic development of the Western world. The television became a consumer object; it discovered its avocation as a domestic rather than public medium within the framework of the developing consumer society of the mid-twentieth century. The development of television is therefore intimately connected with changes in consumer society. The era of scarcity coincides with, and promotes, the development of domestic consumption from its first phase of 'universal provision' to a second phase of growing consumer choice. During the first half of the twentieth century, households became the main market for consumption. They were offered and accepted more and more pieces of equipment, and the use, possession or lack of them became a crucial indicator of social status and class. The provision of electricity was the crucial point of transition. After electricity came vacuum cleaners and refrigerators, radios and electric lamps, washing machines and tumble driers. Technologically, all of these were possible in the 1920s, but their introduction into consumer markets was gradual beyond the United States. Domestic refrigerators were scarce in Britain even in the 1950s. Outside the home stood the car, the crucial mark, in the inter-war years, of middle class status. The nature of the car, too, shows us much about the nature of that commodity market. Henry Ford, the pioneer of cars for the masses, offered 'any colour so long as it's black', a shrewd comment on the nature of commodity provision until relatively late in the twentieth century. It was a matter of manufacturing as many units as possible at a price that a huge mass of individuals could afford. It did not much matter that distinguishing marks were few, and that choice for almost everyone was limited to the models made by a small number of manufacturers.[1] What mattered was the fact of possession: having a car was a crucial mark of status. As consumerism developed, more and more distinctions began to emerge, particularly around the way that the new range of consumer equipment was used. And television played a crucial role in this process.

Television was one of the key signs of growing affluence in the developed world after the Second World War. Television sets first became mass market items in the United States with the continuing boom at the end of the war. Their spread was significantly helped by the growing suburbanization of American society, the zoning of cities and the creation of separate areas of housing with plenty of space.[2] Suburban homes were desirable, but far away from many centres of entertainment. Television offered to bring entertainment into those homes. In Britain, televisions were acquired in their millions early in the 1950s under the twin impetus of the televised coronation of Queen Elizabeth in 1953 and the introduction in 1955 of a popular commercial service to rival the BBC.[3] In other parts of Europe, the acquisition of televisions came slightly later. But in every case, the pattern was the same. The television was one of the first capital items to be acquired, often ahead of a refrigerator or a washing machine. The black and white picture provided unlimited entertainment, so it seemed a particular bargain. In Britain at least, no capital purchase was necessary, since televisions could be rented from companies that provided a repair service into the bargain (a considerable advantage since 'TV repairman' was one of the growth occupations in the period). At one time, the majority of sets in Britain were rented rather than owned. In just five years, satires on this new phenomenon had to adjust to a new social reality. In 1952 the Ealing comedy film *Meet Mr Lucifer* showed how television ruined lives by becoming a social focus: people were always calling round to view the first sets in the neighbourhood. By 1956, the American film *All That Heaven Allows* used the gift of a television to symbolize the lowest point in the social isolation of a widow.

The television changed the households that it entered. It introduced a different way of living and even of organizing the domestic space. The television had to go somewhere, and, as Lynn Spigel shows in her pioneering study *Make Room for TV*, there was a vivid debate in the American magazines – and even in television programmes – about what room was appropriate. One manufacturer even produced a kitchen unit combining a television and an oven so that the housewife could go about her business and watch TV at the same time. Perhaps the only reason why such a hybrid did not appear in Europe was the fact that daytime television, established in America from 1948, was not considered appropriate by European regulators and industry alike until more than thirty years later. Even in the USA, it provoked a vivid debate about whether the housewife could manage her time so that her chores would still get done. American sociologists in the 1940s, according to Spigel, debated whether the television promoted family unity because they viewed together, or repressed conversation and so ruined family life. Others pointed to the problems of bad nutrition caused by eating in front of the television in the family room. This again is a culturally specific question. Jacques Rozier's 1963 film *Adieu Philippine* shows a vivid family argument taking place around the dining table, with the television firmly placed at the head of the table. Such a solution appears not to have been common in America.

Television was also the sign of modernity. It brought the modern world of consumerism and mechanization into the home. Every night its comedies and dramas showed the kinds of lifestyle that others lived. Indeed, one of the crucial early developments of television, according to Spigel, was the situation comedy. The overwhelming majority of these series of half-hour programmes were set in domestic situations, and they showed the adventures of their characters with ordinary domestic appliances. So, for example, they showed how people dealt with the television set, and its not infrequent breakdowns. They showed how traditional characters acted when presented with ultra-modern homes. In short, they provided a flow of conceptions of modern life with its machines and its styles. And the programmes themselves were surrounded by advertisements which showed the potential universe of purchases, the benefits of home mechanization, and the superiority of mass-produced items to the traditional and artisanal. The television was just one of the domestic appliances that was on the market in the post-war period, but it was the crucial one that encouraged purchase of all the others. And it drove the will to work to acquire these items. Television images of modern mechanized affluence were important in encouraging the migration of workers from poor areas like southern Italy towards the industrial north.[4] Commentators who seek to understand the influence of television should perhaps look at its contribution to these profound social changes, rather than seeking a direct alteration of individual responses to stimuli.

The Patterns of the Everyday

Television promoted the modernization of society and the development of a mass consumer society, yet it did so in a particularly
intimate way. Scheduling emerged as broadcasting began to understand that its live nature gave it an intimate relationship with the
everyday lives of its audiences. As Paddy Scannell puts it:

> Broadcasting gathered together a quite new kind of public life – a world
> of public persons, events and happenings – and gave this world an
> orderly, familiar, knowable appearance by virtue of an unobtrusive tem-
> poral sequence of events that gave structure and substance to everyday
> life.[5]

This included the annual round of sporting events; political
rituals like the state openings of parliament, the Chancellor of the
Exchequer's annual budget and the Lord Mayor's banquet; seasonal
fashions and the movements of the aristocracy from town to
country. As a complement to this sequence of events in the public
sphere came a necessity to understand the rhythms of the private
sphere. It became important to know when the various sections of
the population awoke in the morning, took their meals, returned
from work, went to bed. Television moulded itself to the patterns of
everyday life, and in doing so defined and standardized them.
Television's managers, in an inheritance from the habits of radio,
designed the evening output according to an assumed pattern of
average national daily life. So they extrapolated from the assumed
regular rhythms of the household, and established an ordering of
programmes that would be most appropriate. Scannell cites Grace
Wyndham-Goldie's description of the period between six and seven
in the evening which the BBC decided to fill in 1957 with a new kind
of programme, the magazine format *Tonight* which attempted to
respond to the likely activities of its viewers by providing a mixture
of short items:

> There would be coming and going: women getting meals for teenagers
> who were going out and preparing supper for men who were coming in;
> men in the North would be having their tea; commuters in the South
> would be arriving home. There was no likelihood of an audience which
> would be ready to view steadily for half-an-hour at a time.[6]

The staggered return from the outside world, first children, then
the breadwinner, dictated in most of the Western world that chil-

dren's television preceded a main news bulletin. But the precise timing of that bulletin varies widely between nations. It was still crucially determined by mealtimes, and whether television news was seen as an appropriate accompaniment or preparation to the family's evening meal. Similarly, the structure of the schedules mirrored assumptions about the time that the majority of the population were expected to go to bed, which is determined by work start times and the length of the journey to work.

Schedules, too, reflected the rhythms of the year. Paddy Scannell and David Cardiff point out that a secular calendar of sporting events had already been developed by radio, and television was their natural successor. As a result, broadcasting became central in the project of articulating a sense of the national. As Scannell and Cardiff point out, 'the cyclical reproduction, year in and year out, of an orderly and regular progression of festivities, rituals and celebrations'[7] provides the backbone of the BBC's definition of national stability and continuity. As recently as 1992, this idea remained a key part of the BBC's explicit project. The BBC's own defence of its 'role in the new broadcasting age' argued that part of the BBC's 'core role' should be 'to give special prominence to the artistic, sporting and ceremonial events that bring the nation together'.[8] Television in Britain owes a lot to the ceremonial: it was the televised coronation of Queen Elizabeth in 1953 that convinced a generation that they really needed a television set. And public service television has been repaying the debt ever since. Television became the keeper of the national calendar, marking the seasons by a ritualistic round of sporting events and commemorations. The Boat Race, the start of the flat-racing season, the Cup Final, the pattern of cricket test matches were amongst the markers in Britain, and again each country had their own. Beyond this lay the patterns of annual holidays (midsummer for northern Europe, August for the Mediterranean countries), secular celebrations and religious holidays. Christmas demanded weeks of special editions of popular programmes (often recorded during the summer months), and in different countries television adapted its scheduling routine to the annual cycle of religious festivals. Television schedules treated each of them as the opportunity for a variation from the normal pattern of broadcasting, and in doing so enabled television to take on the contours of modern domestic life.

As the television schedule was based on an averaging out of the variety of national domestic life into one pattern, it was a force towards the standardization of everyday life. From radio, it had inherited a sense of when it was most appropriate to show certain kinds of programmes, the optimum time for news, for entertainment and for serious programming. But, unlike radio, television saw itself in many parts of the world as a serious medium to which the audience had to pay full attention. In Norway, when the main evening news on the single channel, NRK, was moved by half an hour, many people complained that they had had to adjust their domestic routines and the time of their evening meal so that they could pay the proper degree of attention to the news at its new time.[9] Television in Europe was seen as a matter for the evenings only, unlike the United States. Television was initially seen as a disruption of the routines of home life and social existence, and its schedules took this into account. The BBC showed programmes for children at 5.00pm, but at 6.00pm it stopped transmission so that children could be sent to bed. This was called 'the toddlers' truce' which lasted until 1957 and the development of *Tonight* described above. In Iceland even into the 1980s there was simply no television on Thursdays at all: this was the day set aside for meetings and social activities of all kinds. Both these cases show how television negotiated itself into the particular patterns of life that it presumed its audiences were leading. In Britain, the anxiety about children getting enough sleep was widespread. The long winter nights of Iceland were beguilingly ideal for a domestic audience. But this was a small society with a strong sense of communal values, fearful of the social isolation and fragmentation that might result from a population gathered around the warm glow of the television set, so space was created for sociability. Since these early years, television's attitude to scheduling has become more and more sophisticated, especially with the arrival of competition between channels, as Chapter 9 demonstrates.

Television's first era was a tremendous achievement. Many of its social effects have already been alluded to, particularly its powerful effect in the modernization and urbanization of society. Television in the era of scarcity was also a powerful instrument of social integration. When most households had a television set, and most countries had just one or two television channels, then a large proportion of the population would watch a programme on one or other of those channels every night. In the case of particularly popular programmes, most of the population could be assumed to be viewing. In Britain, with a population of slightly over 50 million, it was not unusual for the most popular programmes like the comedy duo *Morecambe and Wise* to have an audience of 25 million viewers in the 1960s.[10] Such figures are now limited to the truly exceptional and isolated event like the funeral of Diana, Princess of Wales in September 1997.

The Nation's Private Life

During the era of scarcity, television brought national populations together. From 1956 to 1966 and even later, Britain was a nation with two television channels whose mid-evening programmes were the stuff of the next day's conversation. Programmes could bring an unparalleled experience of witness to the homes of the British population. From the minute gestures of comedy performers through the accidents that often overtook live performances, to increasingly graphic news footage from the Congo or Vietnam wars, television brought its viewers at home in contact with events far from home. The sense of complicity that lurks within the experience of witness could sometimes bring about positive action. A single drama like *Cathy Come Home* in 1966 could spark a national debate about housing problems and provide the impetus for the creation of the pressure group Shelter. This television was a very special phenomenon. It was a pervasive and everyday phenomenon. It was urbane and generalist, able to deal with anything that was important in its world. It had an important national role, unifying the nation around a common television culture. Yet at the same time, it was ephemeral. Its broadcasts reached the nation one night and were hardly ever seen again thereafter. This was the television that used to matter. Each of these central characteristics had positive and negative sides, which contributed to the slight unease with which the medium was regarded by those in power. The everyday, familiar television of the limited channel era was something that the whole household shared or argued over. One television per household was the norm, and decisions about the limited choices available were the source of many rows. For although this television was familiar and present every evening, it had a pseudo-availability that suited the era of mass consumption. The television services might be available, but desired individual programmes were not: they could be seen only when the schedule permitted.

The integration of television into everyday conversations contributed powerfully to television's role in the life of the nation. It provided a shared culture of stories and opinions, updated every night. Characters could be dissected, moral quandaries debated, scandals deplored and jokes savoured together. Television provided a kind of national private life, encouraging all the fierce and slightly embarrassed loyalties that affectionate families produce in their members. This shared culture, of course, was also a normative national culture, shaped by the concerns of public service broadcasting. Radio broadcasting brought together a nation that could recognise the catch phrases from *It's That Man Again* during the Second World War ('Can I do you now, sir?' and so on). Television brought together a nation that shared the entertainment of the variety shows *Sunday Night at the London Palladium* and *The Black and White Minstrel Show* (with what now appears to be the distasteful sight of blacked-up white male singers); the raw drama of the innovative police series *Z-Cars*; the comedy of *Steptoe and Son*; the human interest and suspense of game shows like *Double Your Money* and *Take Your Pick*. It was a nation that shared its outrage at *The Wednesday Play;* recognised itself in *Candid Camera*, and knew what *The Cup Final* was without having to ask which cup, let alone which sport. In the era of scarcity, every nation had its particular favourite television characters and performers. They remain unknown outside the nation's boundaries, but command instant recognition and affection from anyone who watched their national television before the 1980s. Sid Caesar means little in Britain, Arthur Haynes means nothing in the United States but on their home territories, these figures remain legendary. Often they are comedians, usually they include at least one newsreader or interviewer, and always they include game-show hosts with their particular tag-lines. Television in the era of scarcity gave each nation its own private life.

Most television during this era was scarcely memorable, despite the grandiose rhetoric that surrounded the medium. In fact, its very lack of cultural weight was the secret of its success. It could be treated casually by its audiences. Television was user-friendly, not because it provided what you wanted when you wanted it, but because it made no necessary demands. This was the price for the entry of this remarkable new technology into virtually every household in the land. Its unassuming, even diffident, nature enabled each household to reach its own accommodation with the medium. Television was easily domesticated, yet it was not used up and discarded like many other domestic technologies. It settled upon a pattern of repetition (the series format) and renewal (the seasonal schedule) that suited the demands of its domestic audiences. And it always promised a little more than it could deliver. In the words of Beverle Houston, cinema's 'direct role is that the spectator says: "I want the cinema experience again" ... of television we say "I want it as I have never had it".'[11] This was television's other secret. It provided both satisfaction and dissatisfaction at the same time. The era of scarcity saw the development of the routines of the television series, of the multiple versions of the same basic format. This habit, which makes television production a much more industrial process than film-making, also binds it profoundly to its audience. Television is familiar and everyday, and its series return in the same form in the same time slots with a reassuring familiarity. The television set was a powerful modernizing force in the millions of homes it entered during the 1950s and 1960s. And it had to negotiate its way into the heart of the family: it had to gain the intimacy that it now has. Television programming was very carefully constructed to ensure that it maintained its intimacy. Nothing that was too offensive was to be broadcast. From this essential early negotiation came a culture that was condemned as 'bland' by critics, but this was necessary nevertheless if television was to gain a central place in the vast majority of households.

Public Service and Private Life

Many commentators, especially in television's early years, were concerned to point out that television was squandering its immense power for social good. This trend is perhaps most evident in Newt Minow's pronouncement when appointed to chair the Federal Communications Commission in America by President Kennedy in 1961. He declared television to be a 'vast wasteland', and accused broadcasters of 'squandering the public airwaves'.[12] This attitude was typical of the time, and public service broadcasting was explicitly developed in Europe to provide a counterbalance to this tendency in television which was seen as inevitable. Behind it lies a fear of

popular programming as embodying the lowest common denomi-
nator in public taste, together with a disdain for people and companies that make a large amount of money from providing popular
programming. Television was seen to be having 'effects' on its
audiences, 'effects' that could ultimately be measured in terms of
'increased propensity to violence' or 'changes in attitude'. A great
deal of academic study – much of it commissioned by governments
– was undertaken in the attempt to isolate and measure these
effects.[13] Such research was almost always inconclusive, and any
conclusions were hedged around with qualifications. Yet the impression that television was somehow socially harmful remained, and
the debate continued. In the early 1980s when the Italian television
system was deregulated, Europe regarded the rapid and chaotic
process and saw just one thing: housewives doing striptease on
daytime programmes. This incident became a rhetorical gesture in
almost any speech in favour of public service broadcasting during
the period: 'Do you want housewives stripping on television?' was
the common cry. This was the public side of television, which
regarded television as something both awesome and dangerous. It
assumed that the medium had great power – which it undoubtedly
does – but at the same time assumed that ordinary citizens were
unable to come to terms with that power – which is much less
certain, to say the least.

Public service broadcasting was Europe's means of ensuring that
the power of television was not squandered.[14] It was also a way of
managing the scarcity of programme supply in the face of the
tremendous demand that the medium excited. In the United States,
stations and networks were allowed to expanded to fulfill as much of
that demand as possible, with little regulation. European governments, motivated by notions of social justice, sought to control and
shape the development of broadcasting more directly by managing
that demand and controlling the growth of the broadcasting sector.
They justified this through arguments about scarcity of resources,
both of wavelengths available for broadcasting and the level of
development of the consumer economy. They had also realized the
potential of broadcasting as a unifying force, pulling together
individuals, families and groups into a national whole. Through the
ideal of public service broadcasting, broadcasting became another
tool in the construction of the nation state. As such, it joined earlier
forces of social unification: the construction of railways, the standardization of clock time, the drive towards universal literacy, the

standardization of working practices and holiday entitlements, the development of universal suffrage, the development of a national press. These were all very valuable, liberating and enriching aspects of the creation of the nation state, which nevertheless involved the destruction of much of the personal and regional individuality that had preceded them, as well as the wilful marginalization of some minorities. Each provided an element of communality along with an element of necessary standardization. The same can be said of television, except in one crucial respect. Television had an intimacy with the national audience, and was able to address people as individuals amongst many other individuals. Once television became sure of its role, this intimacy provided the means by which politicians could be interrogated by professionals posing as representatives of the audience. Gradually, television in Europe realized that it could serve this role. In Britain, it took the introduction of commercial television to force the BBC away from fawning interviews with politicians where they were asked the most anodyne of questions.[15] Interviewers like Robin Day would begin 'What the public really want to know, Minister is ...'. But in France, direct state control of television guaranteed that such techniques, where permitted, were confined to the questioning of opposition politicians. At its most extreme, the censorship of television news meant that the news broadcast was not live at all. When the small Baltic state of Estonia was part of the Soviet Union, its television news was taped an hour and a half before broadcast so that it could be checked for the slightest critical inflection.[16] This is the most extreme example of a general tendency: that television in the era of scarcity became the prime means by which national governments could communicate effectively with their peoples. Different national arrangements and styles were developed depending on the state of the nation's political culture.

In these circumstances, it is not surprising that television's own view of its role became vastly inflated. It appeared to people working in television that they had a vast power to influence opinions and even events. The experience of witness that television brought into the domestic arena was new and hence unpredictable in its effects. Sometimes it did indeed work to force the pace of social change and to reveal hitherto hidden aspects of society. An episode of Roger Graef's *Police*, an observational documentary for the BBC in 1976, showed the hostile handling of a rape victim by the Thames Valley police. They simply did not believe her story, despite her obvious emotional distress. This programme led directly to changes in police procedure.[17] Yet this same power has also led to the abuse of documentary interviewees on occasion, justified by the concept of 'the greater good'. Television thought it could exploit people because of the supposed benefits to showing their plight to an audience of millions. Some items in the trail-blazing BBC2 documentary series *Man Alive*, edited by Desmond Wilcox from 1965 to 1972, were accused of doing this even at the time. A programme in 1967 about obsessive behaviour, *Living with Fear*, featured a woman with a fear of birds taken to a pigeon-infested London station. In *Not on Speaking Terms* in 1973, a bus fanatic was pilloried for his total inability to appreciate how his hobby was taking over his whole life. In other editions, the experience of witness was used to bring the experience of a convicted paedophile or a man with terminal cancer to the attention of a viewing public. It was exploitation 'of a gentle sort' claims one of the directors, Angela Huth, because 'I always felt you had to protect people from themselves. This was thirty years ago, and I think that nobody knew half as much about television then as they do now. Quite often people didn't realise what they were doing, what could be done with it, and how it would appear on the screen.'[18] This was another aspect of television's era of scarcity: a small group of adepts, the programme-makers, were accumulating practical knowledges of the effects of the process of witness, but these knowledges had no wider currency. In the age of scarcity, television came from an elite, and it remained an honour for anyone outside that elite to be invited to appear on the screen.

Commercial Television and Americanization

To begin with, television developed along the pattern of radio, with television in the United States beginning as a commercial operation, and European television as public service. However, there were exceptions. Spain's television service which opened in 1956 was a new form: state-controlled, yet financed mostly from advertising. Governments everywhere assumed the right to control this new and scarce resource. So the American government licensed local television stations and allowed them to take programmes from central production organizations, the networks. In Brazil, the civilian government of the day allowed Roberto Marinho's TV Globo to develop a dominant position in broadcasting during the 1960s, a position that was enhanced through the following military dictatorships. In a country with limited literacy, Marinho was being granted a powerful privilege, which he used to the full. Coverage of political events in periods of democracy was weighted towards the candidates favoured by Marinho. Even in the 1990s, Globo's average audience share was around 70 per cent and its share of the lucrative television advertising market was greater than that.[19] In most of Europe, governments added television to the existing state radio monopolies, giving television a substantial public service role.[20]

Where commercial television did develop, there were still important distinctions to be made. In the United States, television programmes were sponsored, which meant that advertisers paid for their production in return for frequent mentions of their products. Indeed, many of the first programmes to be made for American television were made by the advertisers themselves. The term 'soap opera' derives from the activities of the detergent manufacturers Procter and Gamble in programme-making.[21] Other advertisers favoured a different approach: the spot advertisement inserted between programmes or in breaks within the programmes, but without a close connection with the programme content. Quickly it was realized that this system had its advantages: it avoided the ridiculous situation which occurred when an American gas company required the removal of all references to 'gas' in a programme it was sponsoring about the Nazi death camps in the Second World War.[22] So when commercial television came to public service Europe, with the opening of ITV in Britain in 1955, it carried spot advertisements only, and a new television art form was born.

With commercial television came the threat of American culture, which the public service system thought that it had successfully kept at bay. For whereas it had played a pioneering role in radio, the United States seemed to lag behind Europe in the development of television. In the 1930s, it seemed that American citizens might be offered no less than four networks to choose from, all linked to existing broadcasting or equipment manufacturing companies. The resultant squabbles about technical standards led to the comparatively late launch of television in the United States, and enabled the BBC to pioneer the first regular broadcast service which was launched in 1936. By the outbreak of war in 1939, when the service was closed, it was still broadcasting to a few thousand sets only. But it had set the pattern. The broadcast schedule had a wider range of material than BBC radio (jazz music, which John Reith had banned on radio, was broadcast in 1937), and all the broadcasts, except material bought from film distributors, were live. Another successful (but irregular) TV service had been opened in Germany in March 1935 and it succeeded in broadcasting from the Olympic Games of 1936.[23]

Television was a live medium in the United States when it was eventually launched in 1940. But the sheer problems of American geography necessitated a compromise with the practice of live programming. A show from New York at 7.00pm, the beginning of primetime, would be live in Los Angeles at 4.00pm because of time zone differences. So a rough and ready recording device had to be developed (video-tape was an invention of the late 1950s). A film camera was pointed at a TV set, producing a copy of the live broadcast that could be shown three hours later in California. From this, it was not long before the enterprising producers of *The Lucy Show* hit upon the idea of filming their programmes rather than broadcasting them live, providing the opportunity to edit out mistakes, smooth over transitions and come out with a programme that could be shown more than once.[24] The success of this strategy is demonstrated by the fact that *The Lucy Show* and its successors are still regularly screened around the world. The world market in television programmes had been born.

In that same moment, the argument about 'Americanization' or 'globalization' of television culture was born. Politicians, cultural commentators and religious leaders in Europe all deplored the appearance of American programmes on their television screens, often bought by the upstart commercial channels when they were eventually permitted to begin.[25] This sharpened the existing debate about what interests or individuals were fit to be given the right to own and run television companies, a debate that continues. The regulation of television and the debate about Americanization go hand in hand. This debate was a new phenomenon. There had been no real international market in radio programmes, but filmed or recorded television programmes were extensively traded. The problem with the debate was that 'America' stood for many things in Europe and the rest of the world: for the extensive modernization of society; for the abolition of older social relationships in favour of market relationships; for a liberal attitude to sexual and family relations; for a democratic style of life; for a society in which gun-ownership was legal and violent crime a fact of urban life; for a standard of living that was simply unattainable by many of the world's regions and economies. Television brought all of this into the homes of peoples around the world, so it was not surprising that television became the focus for many national concerns about undesirable social change. As a result, the ownership of commercial television stations became a crucial issue and of close interest to politicians of all tendencies.

The British debate about commercial television took place between 1950 and 1954, and provoked some strange alliances which are typical of the way in which television as a social phenomenon became the focus of many concerns. Initially promoted by those who had the most to gain from it, the advertising industry, the manufacturers of branded everyday consumer goods, and sections of the entertainment industry, the campaign for commercial broadcasting attracted support from some prominent members from the left of the Labour Party. They were in principle against the 'Americanization' in most of its aspects, but favoured the modernizing tendencies of commercial television in one crucial respect. It would provide a place for the popular culture that was excluded from the public service regime of the BBC. They wanted to see a television service that was less 'stuffy' than the BBC. They sought a service that would not give people what would be good for them, but rather would give them more of what they wanted. They wanted television that came from the people, rather than television that was imposed upon them. They knew that there existed a vibrant culture of popular music, jazz, and comedy that was not fully represented on the BBC. They also knew, or had grown up within, regional cultures whose strong accents excluded them from the 'standard English' of the BBC. So the campaign for commercial television in Britain attracted considerable support from the more populist-minded of politicians and commentators from across the political spectrum.[26] And the question of regional cultures assumed a great importance in this debate. Commercial television in Britain was eventually defined in law as a regional television service to counter the national service of the BBC. As originally designed by parliament, commercial television was intended to give each geographical region of the country its own television service. This was a result of an explicit criticism of the BBC for being too London-based and too concerned with the high culture of the more affluent classes. ITV (Independent Television) as it was called, was intended to counter the unwanted effects of the public service regime of the BBC. It was to present regional culture as opposed to national culture, and to be run by regional business interests as opposed to the national state-owned BBC.

It did not work out quite like this in practice. The project was at once out of date and ahead of its time. It was ahead of its time in terms of television. The idea of regionally based broadcasting is more typical of the second age of broadcasting, the age of availability, in which many countries, even as small as Denmark (with a population of 5 million and a small land mass), have regionally based television services. But in the era of scarcity, television worked with larger and less differentiated audiences, and so its programmes became a part of national life. The idea that each region of Britain should have its own programmes organized in its own schedule caused problems for the audience who saw it as somehow marginal and isolating compared to the unifying BBC. It also caused problems for advertisers. Most were concerned with supporting a national rather than a regional market, and preferred a television service that reflected this. The project was out of date from their point of view, reflecting a nostalgia for the local which the consumer capitalism of the period was sweeping away. In the end, though, it was the sheer economics of television production that forced ITV to change. It proved simply too expensive to support the production of a full television service in eight different regional centres. After a year, the pioneering companies presented an ultimatum: either we can form a network, each providing programmes from the others to show all at the same time, or we close down entirely.[27] So regional television became a muted and marginal characteristic of ITV rather than a defining one.

However, ITV's mobilization of popular culture and American culture was far more successful, despite the initial intentions of the regulatory authority, the Independent Television Authority, which had refused to give a licence to the show-business mogul Lew Grade. British audiences were given American-style game shows featuring British working class contestants. They saw American situation comedies and westerns. They had many more variety shows featuring routinely the kinds of acts that had been a rarity on BBC television, including *Cool for Cats* (1956-61), a record-based rock'n'roll series. They were given increasing amounts of fiction made within the then popular genres of the western (*Gunsmoke* from the USA in 1956) and swashbuckling melodrama (like the British-produced *The Buccaneers* from 1956), as well as genres that remain fashionable like the American crime series *Dragnet*. They were given from 1960 a soap opera, *Coronation Street*, set in what was then a typical street of urban terraced housing in Manchester. 'The Street' became one of the cornerstones of popular British television. In this context, the BBC faced a crisis. On many evenings, three quarters of the audience were not watching the BBC at all. So the BBC was forced to redefine its public service mission in relation to commercial competition, and it has been doing so ever since. The BBC adopted and developed many of the genres of popular broadcasting. It took the new democratic tone of ITV news and made *Tonight*, British television's first news magazine which mixed serious and human interest stories in short items held together by a team of eccentric reporters. It took the already popular comedian Tony Hancock and fashioned a situation comedy around him where he no longer responded explicitly to the studio audience with repartee as he had done, but simply used their laughter to hone his comic timing. At the same time, the BBC was careful to maintain and develop the kinds of programmes that commercial television shied away from: the poetic documentaries of Denis Mitchell like *Morning in the Streets* (1959), the big budget cultural series like *Civilisation* (1969), innovative drama like *The Forsyte Saga* (1967) and *The Six Wives of Henry VIII* (1970). The BBC's response to commercial competition in the era of scarcity was measured rather than imitative. However, it is clear that public service television only found its public when commercial television began to steal it away.

This story was repeated throughout Europe over the following thirty years, and the terms of the debate are remarkably similar. On the one side lay a public service television whose primary ethos was one of national unity, whose aims were the education, information and improvement of the population. Entertainment was conceived as a means of achieving these aims, as a necessary envelope for these more important messages. Against this ethos was an unstable coalition of regional interests, populist tendencies and entertainment interests, allied with companies concerned with developing the consumer market. The last nation in democratic Europe to satisfy this populist coalition was Norway, with the launch of TV2 in 1992. Elsewhere, the process happened much earlier, but always the commercial television services were required to satisfy significant conditions in their programme provision. They too had to provide news even though it was expensive and by no means popular. They too had to provide documentaries when game shows, soap operas and imported series would guarantee them a larger audience with less effort and, sometimes, less antagonism of political and social groups. Television in the age of scarcity was always to be a regulated television, with regulation increasingly seen as the necessary price for its social power and ubiquity.

The era of scarcity was also the era in which television's basic pattern of genres was developed, along with its significant regional variants. The global trade in television programmes did, as predicted, develop in this period as a trade dominated by American productions. Many European public service broadcasters, whilst publicly deploring this tendency, nevertheless sent its key production personnel to America to learn the techniques of the sort of popular generic television they were developing.[28] The genre of the situation comedy was one such example, where the techniques of multi-camera recording pioneered on such series as *The Lucy Show* in 1950 were still novel a decade later in the UK when they were adopted for *Hancock's Half Hour*. Audiences saw American product, and in large parts of the world, they liked what they saw. After all, this was the same industry that had dominated many of the world's cinema screens since the First World War had virtually destroyed the powerful European film industries[29] But even in this period of scarcity, dominated internationally by American production, significant regional markets were growing. American production only replaced local production in places where economic conditions made its development unrealistic: small Pacific island states, for instance, or the poorer parts of Africa. Everywhere else, American production took its place alongside local production, where the fact of local languages, personalities and cultures gradually made a local television culture. If television in the age of scarcity provided the private life of the nation, the American product tended to provide the dreams and the nightmares, leaving the more comfortable, the more intimate and the more everyday moments to local production. Significant alternative circuits of distribution began to develop, and with them their distinctive genres. Brazil, Mexico and to a lesser extent Argentina developed the distinctive genre of the TV novella, which lies somewhere between a vastly extended serial and a truncated soap opera, and is played in an emotional key that contrasts strongly to both the social realism of British soaps and the nervous energy of American or Australian soaps.[30] Novellas found a wide market both within and outside Latin America, providing a significant cultural counter-weight to American production even in the era of television scarcity.

The era of television scarcity was bound not to continue. Pressures from within the industry itself in all its significant markets would alone have driven the expansion of television. But the television industry was in a significant way public property, a central feature of the everyday life of every nation that had television. So the way that television changed from this first era to the second era, that of availability, was defined by far wider social currents. These social currents had themselves been encouraged and even shaped by television itself, so the story is a double-sided one, of influences given and influences received. This befits such an important medium.

---

[1] David Harvey, *The Condition of Postmodernity* (Oxford: Basil Blackwell, 1990) is a good source of information on this subject, in particular Part II, 'The Political-economic transformation of late twentieth-century capitalism'.

[2] See Roger Silverstone, *Television and Everyday Life* (London: Routledge, 1994) and Lynn Spigel, *Make Room for TV: Television and the Family Ideal in Postwar America* (Chicago: University of Chicago Press, 1992).

[3] On this point, see p 56 of John Corner's 'General introduction' to his *Popular Television in Britain: Studies in Cultural History* (London: British Film Institute, 1991).

[4] See Eric Hobsbawm, *Age of Extremes: The Short Twentieth Century 1914-1991* (London: Michael Joseph, 1994), Chapter 9, 'The Golden Years', pp 257-86, and also the BBC documentary series *People's Century* ('1948 Boom Time').

[5] Paddy Scannell, *Radio, Television and Modern Life: A Phenomenological Approach* (Oxford: Basil Blackwell, 1996), p 153.

[6] *Ibid.*, p 150.

[7] Paddy Scannell and David Cardiff, *A Social History of British Broadcasting, 1922-1939* (Oxford: Basil Blackwell, 1991).

[8] BBC Corporate Affairs, *Extending Choice* (London: BBC, 1992), p 21.

[9] See Trine Syvertsen, *Public Television in Transition*, Levender Bilder 5 (Oslo: KULT/NAVE, 1992).

[10] Such figures are extrapolated from data for the number of homes watching provided by TAM (Television Audience Measurement Ltd). So a high rating episode of *Coronation Street*, for example, was seen on Wednesday 24 January 1965 by 9.66 million homes.

[11] Beverle Houston, 'Viewing television: the metapsychology of endless consumption', *Quarterly Review of Film Studies* 9/3 (1984), pp 183-95.

[12] Minow challenged broadcasting executives to 'sit down in front of your television set when your station goes on the air ... and keep your eyes glued to that set until the station signs off. I can assure you that you will observe a vast wasteland.' Quoted from Horace Newcomb (ed), *An Encyclopedia of Television*, vol 2 (Chicago and London: Fitzroy Dearborn, 1997), pp 1057-8.

[13] Two noteworthy sources are David Gauntlett's section on 'The state of effects research' in his *Moving Experiences: Understanding Television's Influences and Effects* (London: John Libbey and Company Ltd, 1995), pp 9-12, and Dr Guy Cumberbatch's chapter on 'Violence and the mass media: the research evidence' in Guy Cumberbatch and D. Howitt, *A Measure of Uncertainty: The Effects of Mass Media* (London: John Libbey and Company Ltd, 1989), pp 31-59.

[14] For an account of public service broadcasting in Europe, see Patrick Humphreys, *Mass Media and Media Policy in Western Europe* (Manchester: Manchester University Press, 1996).

[15] A succinct analysis of ITV's innovative approach to news and current affairs (and the BBC's response to it) is provided by Andrew Crisell in pages 91-4 of *An Introductory History of British Broadcasting* (London: Routledge, 1997).

[16] My source is a conversation with a former employee of the Estonian television news service.

[17] See Jeanne Gregory and Sue Lees, *Policing Sexual Assault* (London: Routledge, 1999), and *Guardian*, G2 supplement, 1 March 1999, p 6.

[18] See *Man Alive*, a 'Late Show' documentary, BBC2, August 1993.

[19] See Roberto Mader, 'Globo Village: television in Brazil' in Tony Dowmunt (ed), *Channels of Resistance* (London: British Film Institute, 1993) and *Brazil: Beyond Citizen Kane* directed by Simon Hartog, Channel 4 TV, 1993.

[20] Spain is the major exception to this rule.

[21] 'Most network [radio] soap operas were produced by advertising agencies, and some were owned by the sponsoring client.' Robert C. Allen in Horace Newcomb (ed), *Encyclopedia of Television*, vol 3 (Chicago: Fitzroy Dearborn, 1997), p 1518. Also, see William Boddy, *Fifties Television: The Industry and its Critics* (Urbana: University of Illinois Press, 1990) and Christopher Anderson, *Hollywood Television: The Studio System in the Fifties* (Austin: University of Texas Press, 1994).

[22] Francis Wheen uses this example in his *Television* (London: Century, 1985), of the American Gas Association sponsoring a programme entitled *Judgement at Nuremberg*, in which all references to the use of gas chambers in the Holocaust were edited out of the final programme. Done at a late stage in the production, this inevitably left unexplained pauses in the narration.

[23] See Albert Abramson, 'The invention of television' in Anthony Smith (ed), *Television: An International History* (Oxford: Oxford University Press, 1995), p 29.

[24] See Anderson: *Hollywood Television*.

[25] See Dick Hebdige's 'Towards a cartography of taste 1935-1962' in his *Hiding in the Light* (London: Routledge, 1988). That this was a clear concern during the debate surrounding the introduction of commercial television in Britain is acknowledged by H.H. Wilson in *Pressure Group: The Campaign for Commercial Television* (London: Secker & Warburg, 1961), p 183: '[Conservative MPs] offered assurances that nothing would be done to harm the BBC and that British sponsored television would not be anything like that in the United States. There would be controls and, in any case, British taste was superior to the American and would never tolerate abuses.'

[26] See, for example, Wilson: *Pressure Group* or p 284 of Asa Briggs, *The BBC: The First Fifty Years* (Oxford: Oxford University Press, 1985).

[27] For further details, see Bernard Sendall, *Independent Television in Britain*, vol 1 (London: Macmillan, 1982), pp 326-9.

[28] See Jerome Bourdon, 'The early Americanisation of European television: America as a professional resource', paper given at the Media History Conference, University of Westminster, July 1998.

[29] For the film industry, see Kristin Thompson, *Exporting Entertainment: America in the World Film Market* 1907-1934 (London: British Film Institute, 1985), and for television see Anderson: *Hollywood Television.*

[30] Further information on Latin American novellas can be found in Michele and Armand Mattelart, *The Carnival of the Images: Brazilian Television Fiction* (New York: Bergin & Garvey, 1990), and Mader: 'Globo Village'.

CHAPTER 5

THE SECOND ERA OF TELEVISION: AVAILABILITY

By the end of the twentieth century, television had left behind the era of scarcity. Even in nations with relatively few television channels in the local market, satellite transmission across national borders and local cable services in urban areas had ensured that a significant part of the audience had access to several if not many channels. The huge public demand for television that had been kept in check in the era of scarcity was finally being met. Television moved into an era of availability, where a choice of pre-scheduled services existed at every moment of the day and night. An era of plenty, in which choice would not depend upon the schedules of television transmission, had been envisaged during this period, but remained a commercial dream at the end of the century.[1] The era of scarcity was replaced by managed choice. The mutually dependent competition between one public service channel and its commercial rival, which was typical of the age of scarcity in Europe, gave way to the competition between several providers of markedly different character. Public service broadcasters began to lose confidence dramatically, but by the end of the century it seemed that they were finding a new role. In the United States, the stable structure of four commercial networks that characterized the era of scarcity gave way to a multitude of channels, delivered mainly by cable, with which the four established networks (joined in the mid-1990s by a fifth, The Fox Network) were eventually to command just half the viewing audience. Just like the public service networks in Europe, the American networks suffered from a drastic loss of confidence during this period, despite their continued dominance of many areas of production.[2]

Television developed into this era of its history during the 1980s, at a time when the world was changing around it. The post-war settlement had provided ideological certainty as well as material security. This was the era of the Cold War, a global stand-off between the victorious powers of the Second World War which divided the world into three zones of interest: the West, the Soviet bloc and the Third World. The division between the West and the Soviet bloc was as solid in the mind as it was on the ground. Physical boundaries like the Berlin Wall separated contrasting ideologies which struggled to contain the aspirations of their populations. The Third World was the zone of ambiguity and residual turmoil, where wars were fought because war was impossible between the West and the Soviet bloc, except in the form of global annihilation. This was a global division in which everyone knew where they stood: a permanent stand-off to replace the ideological turmoil of the pre-war era and prevent, so we thought, the recurrence of the genocide of the Second World War. This secure stasis was the first time that a coherent and unified global landscape had been created. It was the landscape of science fiction, stark in its crude divisions, but real enough for all that. It did not collapse with the Berlin Wall, that moment of pseudo-triumph of West over East, when sections of the press were able to announce 'the end of history'.[3] The collapse of the nervous certainty of the post-war years took place messily on the streets of Vukovar and Sarajevo, when history and difference returned to Europe in their ugliest form. Such vicious local conflicts, drawing on submerged differences, had never really gone away; they had simply been confined to Third World countries as various as the Congo, Chile and East Timor.

Consumption and Difference

The certainties of this extraordinary period have now vanished. Yet the distinctive Western economy which developed during this period continues to grow. Its particular form, its culture of consumption, has in many ways created the world in which we now live: the world of multiple and multiplying differences. A fundamental shift took place in economic and ideological life alike, and developments in communication were central to this change. During the period from the 1970s onwards, Western societies moved out of the era of mass markets for standardized consumer products. The emerging new era uses a global market to offer a wider and wider range of differing products and differing versions of the same product to consumers who are more discriminating and more fragmented. The Fordist standardization of commodities for a national market is being replaced by a post-Fordist model. Products are made in one place for global distribution to specific groups of consumers. This is a double process, at once global and local. Thanks to the process of 'flexible specialization' as the economist Robin Murray has called it,[4] they can be made in relatively small numbers rather than in the huge runs associated with the mass consumer markets of the earlier part of this century. Yet these goods find their purchasers on a world market, in many different places, and are used by consumers to define their identities as individual consumers with a special sense of style. Commodity production is increasingly aimed at providing people with the means of establishing their distinctiveness from each other rather than their communality with each other. Commodities now come in an increasing number of different guises: in special editions; different packaging; decorated with logos; or with subtly differentiated design. What matters now is 'style'.

Any differentiation between social groups, however slight, can become significant in this process. The market itself is engaged on a project of giving significance to differences. It presents consumers with choices, linked to senses of self and self-worth, where once they had needs, generated by the struggle to survive and to live comfortably. In the middle years of the century, commodity purchase and use had connoted differences in class, in social position and in cultural aspiration. The video recorder and the satellite dish were perhaps the last such commodities to be introduced. Charlotte Brunsdon has shown how the satellite dish carried a 'working class' or 'culturally

inferior' connotation.⁵ Yet both the satellite dish and the video
recorder were harbingers of this new development of consumerism,
one that brought increasing choice to the huge and relatively pros-
perous urban populations of the second half of the twentieth
century.

For the twentieth-century population explosion itself made possible
this development of individual differentiation. Interests and behaviours that were once considered just personal oddities or eccentrici-
ties have become significant identities to which marketing can be
addressed. This qualitative change in the nature of society is the
result of the combination of growth in population and communications. All individuals in a crowded world seek to define themselves
and to mark themselves out from the anonymity of the crowd by
developing such interests and the pleasures and conviviality that they
provide. Anyone with an abiding interest in anything, from the
character of birdsong to fetishistic sex, can find plenty of other
people with similar interests, forming both a social network and a
potential market. Inter-personal forms of communication, of which
the telephone was the first model, allow individuals to associate
relatively freely with each other. The development of the Internet as a
huge forum for such encounters is just the most recent example of
this tendency. Behind the 'information society' lies this deep human
need for association and personal fulfilment, as like-minded individuals try to find each other and to satisfy their needs across the
increasingly complex universe of human activity.

Each specialized taste or need forms small potential markets
within each nation state that can be reached only by a diversified
culture of communication and marketing. More targeted forms of
marketing, taking place through a multiplicity of channels, are able to
reach them and address them as particular citizens. And the global
communication of money in electronic form enables each market to
flourish wherever its fragments are located geographically. Markets
have become at once global and particular. The nation state is left
somewhat uneasily marooned between the two. It was a crucial
factor in creating the market conditions for the marketing of commodities, but that process has now outrun the nation state itself.
During the heyday of its success, the nation state accumulated too
many functions to itself. Now that the nation state's role as the
principal focus of market standardization has become redundant to a
significant degree, the forces that it managed to repress are beginning
to reassert themselves. Some of these functions strain to become

global rather than national; others cry out to be localized either geographically or into particular social groups or alliances. All of this has created acute problems for the idea of public service broadcasting which developed in television's era of scarcity.

At the level of individuals, the new consumerism is one of multiple and shifting identifications. Within this market of ever more differentiated and targeted commodities, it sometimes seems that individuals can establish their styles and identities from a vast range of possibilities. This has been the subject of one strand of the postmodernist critique of society that identifies a 'pick and mix' attitude to styles. There is certainly some descriptive truth in this. As citizens we are now used to identifying ourselves with fragments of society rather than with the increasingly mythical 'mass'. We inhabit many different identities: we are male or female; young or old or middle-aged; yuppies or comfortable couples or aspirant or making do; we are gay or straight or ambivalent or celibate; sick or well or in between. We belong to particular cities and regions; to ethnic groups and to particular families; to religious and political organizations. We have tastes in food and entertainment, in clothing and transport; we are parents and children. Yet while some of these are choices, others are at the cores of our identities. And while we are more and more aware of belonging to a range of interest groups and like-minded people, we are, conversely, aware of not belonging to others. We are equally aware that our range of choices and our particular identity differs from that of almost everyone around us. We participate in the myriad of differences that exist in society, and form our distinctive individualities from amongst them. Marketing techniques have been developing over many years towards the identification and servicing of these different social groups and the people who identify parts of themselves with them. In Britain, the first moves in this direction were probably in the late 1950s, with the recognition of a specific social group called 'teenagers', whose identifiable tastes and spending power marked them out from all other social groups. As the century closed, the BBC initiated a large-scale internal exercise aimed at defining its new audiences. It was entitled 'The Hundred Tribes of Britain'.[6]

Now the techniques of targeting are far more sophisticated than those of the mid-century. Marketing routinely works with a huge palette of different consumer interests. Commitment to one product is often taken as an indication of interest in a further matching range of products. If you eat take-away pizzas regularly, then the market researchers can identify you with a bundle of other likely consumer choices: rented videos; CD purchases; clothing from Next or Gap; purchase of a customized new Ford; readership of the *Daily Mail*; package holidays to the Mediterranean or Florida. This profile of a typical purchaser is then used to construct tie-in offers (for example, 'Buy two Pizza Hut pizzas and get a Blockbuster video hire voucher'), thus reinforcing the process. Of course both Pizza Hut and Blockbuster are transnational brands operated by one corporation or licensed to local operators. The point is that each brand is targeted towards particular consumer profiles. The transnational corporate structure enables the cross-promotion of these brand-identities to take place. The vast palette of consumer interests is mixed and matched to create likely colour schemes. This is a predictive rather than analytic science, aimed at influencing future buying habits rather than analysing the present, let alone investigating the past. Market research interrogates consumer choices and constructs consumer profiles in order to influence the shifting surfaces of lifestyles. It is interested in social movements only to the extent that they will influence consumer choices and create new market opportunities.[7]

Difference: Style or Substance?

All of this effort aims to produce more and more differentiation between people. These differences have to be made significant in order to provide fresh market opportunities for commodities that will confirm or express identities established from out of those differences. Our modern economy is profoundly interested in social difference. But there is a price that is now being paid for this increasing social differentiation. Not all these differences are trivial and decorative; some are fundamental, and lead to new forms of social conflict. Indeed, Western and even world societies since the 1960s have become increasingly concerned with social conflict and confrontation. The everyday lives of citizens now bring them into contact with people, ideas and behaviours that are difficult to comprehend. Sometimes they are difficult to tolerate as well, and sometimes directly offensive. Spike Lee's film of 1989, *Do The Right Thing*, provides a vivid example of this process, showing a New York street where different behaviours and ethnic cultures co-exist in the same space yet have little to do with each other. The emblematic figure of a character with a 'boom-box', surrounding himself with the noise of his music, provides the final social irritant that makes mutual tolerance and indifference tip over into violent confrontation. The question of race, the essentialization of behaviours into matters of colour and genetics, immediately rushes in to provide a convenient structure for the conflict. Such, says Lee, is the nature of modern society, but he, like everyone else, is unable to propose a way of improving things apart from 'more tolerance'. The modern city offers a huge range of choices of lifestyle, and of people who have chosen to live in particular ways, or who are quite happy with the cultures into which they were born. Yet the same space encloses them all, and their actions often lead to antagonisms of various kinds. This is the other reality of an economic system that provides its citizens with choice, and encourages the increasing sub-division of choice as a means of establishing and developing personal identity. Not all personal identity choices are benign.

Recent work by cultural theorists like Paul Gilroy in *The Black Atlantic* and Homi K. Bhabha in *The Location of Culture* provides new means of thinking through these questions, and specifically the nature of cultural diversity, difference and their attendant problems. It is no coincidence, then, that both writers identify themselves as part of the black diaspora, and Gilroy in particular seeks to place this diaspora at the centre of the stage of modern history rather than in the wings. The urgency of such an argument to our current situation can be gauged from the following:

> ... the universality and rationality of enlightenment in Europe and America were used to sustain and relocate rather than to eradicate an order of racial difference inherited from the premodern era. ... In this setting, it is hardly surprising that if it is perceived to be relevant at all, the history of slavery is somehow assigned to blacks. It becomes our special property rather than a part of the ethical and intellectual heritage of the West as a whole.[8]

In exploring the inheritance of slavery, Gilroy demonstrates the inadequacy of most conventional responses to the problem of racial and cultural difference in the contemporary world. Such differences certainly cannot be treated as discrete since they interact daily, and are caught in a continuing process of redefinition. Neither can they be seen as able to settle side-by-side; nor can they be given the liberal treatment of inclusion in a vast rainbow coalition of progressive

elements. There are irreducible antagonisms involved. In using the
term 'diaspora', Gilroy is well aware that a deep hostility towards
Jews exists within black communities, particularly in the USA. The
importance of Gilroy's work, and the optimistic perspective that
begins to emerge from it, lies in his exploration of the nature of this
irreducible antagonism.

Gilroy's examination of the appeal of black music reveals the
nature of the antagonism. Black music from the United States has a
tremendous hold over the global imagination of the second half of
the twentieth century. Much of this music consists of

> love stories or more appropriately love and loss stories. That they as-
> sume this form is all the more striking because the new genre seems to
> express a cultural decision not to transmit details of the ordeal of slavery
> openly in story and song. Yet these narratives of love and loss system-
> atically transcode other forms of yearning and mourning associated with
> histories of dispersal and exile and the remembrance of unspeakable
> terror.[9]

Gilroy seems to be indicating that the 'universal' appeal of the
music is felt by a world which has been forced to witness elements
of the same terrors, not so much at first hand, but rather through
film and television. This is music for those who cannot say that they
did not know; for those who have felt the pull of complicity with
events that they have witnessed yet can scarcely comprehend. Yet he
stresses other elements of black culture which are also bound up in
the same 'cultural decision not to transmit details of the ordeal of
slavery openly'. Specifically,

> an amplified and exaggerated masculinity [which] has become the boast-
> ful centrepiece of a culture of compensation that self-consciously salves
> the misery of the disempowered and subordinated. This masculinity and
> its relational feminine counterpart become special symbols of the differ-
> ence that race makes.[10]

The world to which the music appeals has more difficulty with
many aspects of this masculinity. It is antagonistic to the way that
many people live their lives; it is particularly antagonistic to anyone
informed by a feminist perspective; and at street level its characteristic styles are perceived as threatening, even when no threat is
intended.

Behind all of this, too, there lies the fundamental reproach to
Western society of the existence of the black diaspora, the legacy of
slavery. At the basis of all our universal concepts, of the establish-

ment of rationality and democracy, of the belief in progress and even the perfectibility of the human, lies the fact of the racially based slavery which enabled the enlightenment to unfold itself. It is an act of extraordinary collective forgetting, of tremendous intellectual hypocrisy, that this has only recently been established as the structuring absence of Western philosophy. So Gilroy identifies three elements here, all indissolubly linked. The first is an element of universal appeal, rooted in the experience of slavery. The second is a series of behaviours with the same root which are far more difficult for many to cope with. Beneath both of these lies a difference in perspective that undermines some of the certainties of Western culture. All come together; all have to be negotiated. Along with the 'enriching' elements come the irreducible antagonisms and the fundamental challenges. Such is the nature of world culture as the new millennium dawns. The same analysis could be made for each of the major sectors of difference: be they gender,[11] sexual orientation, religion or culture. These differences cannot be reduced to a single unity since they all involve elements that are antagonistic to one another. There can be no rainbow coalition; nor can there be a real national unity. The end of history has not taken place as predicted. On the contrary, history bears down on the present as it is a key component in providing the differences that the market is intent on developing.

Difference and National Unity

These developments present particular problems for the nation state, the arena in which broadcasting itself developed. The global economy is reducing the importance of the nation state, as it is becoming at once more global and more highly individualized. The market consists of a system of commodity production that uses social differentiation and the creation of ever more sophisticated ways of signifying individuality as the motor for economic growth. This has a social cost, which is felt at the level of the nation state: social antagonisms that are more difficult to contain within notions of national unity. Faced with burgeoning differences, it is increasingly difficult for the nation state to pick up 'the scraps, patches and rags of daily life', as Homi K.Bhabha puts it,[12] and sew them together into

a national flag. The way in which any one person identifies themselves as a 'national' of a particular nation is at best merely one of the
possible identifications available for the modern process of identity-
building; and it is not one that lends itself very easily to commodifi-
cation either. Once you have stuck the national flag as a logo on a
range of products, and marketed a few 'typical' products to tourists,
there is nothing much left to do. Identification as a 'national citizen'
is increasingly difficult for anyone caught in the vast web of identifications that are to some degree antagonistic to the nation state. With
the increasing valuation of fragments, of local identities, of repressed
elements, the unifying project of the nation state becomes ever more
difficult to achieve.

The end of the century has seen the nation state attempting to
respond to these challenges in a number of ways. In Britain, the state
has gathered ever more power to itself: spectacularly so during the
Thatcher era of the 1980s. In many contexts, we can see the emergence of the most virulent and ugly manifestations of nationalism.
Every kind of difference that nation-building has seized upon is now
caught up into exclusivisms: race, territory, religion, colour, language,
blood, lifestyle, sexual orientation, physical ability. Any difference
that exists between people can be exploited by this hysterically
defensive nationalism. This is nationalism trying to regain for its own
purposes the very social movement that is undermining it. Nevertheless, the nation state remains a necessary structure. The consequences of the new market-place of social identities is felt at the level
of the nation state simply because these different identities inhabit
the same space on earth, and the nation state is still the main arena
for the negotiation and arbitration between conflicting social groups.
As a form of political regulation of a physical area in which social
conflicts have to be resolved, the nation state has a continuing role.
The limits of acceptable communal behaviour have to be continually
established and then enforced if any form of physical co-existence is
to remain possible. The alternative is simple: a society composed of
ghettos for rich and poor alike, a vision which is already emerging in
the so-called United States of America.[13] To prevent this from
developing, a degree of consensus has to be developed, similar to the
consensus that Gramsci described, which serves to bind together
civil society.[14] But it will have to be a continually renegotiated
consensus. This consensus will be established between the major
groupings within the boundaries of the nation state (or within other
such communities), but will belong to no one of those groups.

Crucial here are shared conventions of communication. Everyday social encounters are becoming more and more mystifying as society continues to diversify itself by multiplying its significant differences. For example, styles of speech and physical address have so diversified in Britain that a branch of counselling has developed to mediate between parties who misunderstand each other. A new profession of trainers in self-presentational skills has emerged to develop skills in the correct or required forms of behaviour for particular social exchanges. Increasing social fragmentation is one possible consequence of the new market-place of identities.

Television has played its part in promoting this new market. Television provided the means by which the increasing multiplication of consumer possibilities was paraded before viewing nations, just as it had done in the earlier period of modernization and development of the consumer market. Television provided the advertisements, television provided the entertainment material which showed new lifestyle possibilities. Yet at the same time television has been changed by that process. Television reconstructed itself to incorporate increasing choice, and to cater for the increasingly diverse demands of its viewers. In almost every country in the world, more television channels were opened from the 1970s onwards, forcing changes in the way that television was regulated, and, more importantly, in the way that television related to its audiences. A television regime of two or three channels is fundamentally different from a regime of four or five. In a two or three channel regime, the choice on offer is limited by complementarity, in which each channel will usually seek at any one moment to offer a different type of programme to those on offer on the other channels. The assumption is that the audience is a mass audience with relatively few differentiations. Once more than three or four channels exist, more nuanced notions of the audience begin to develop. The audience is conceived as much more a loose assemblage of minorities to be brought into various kinds of coalition, or even to be addressed singly. The mode of address of programmes begins to change, becoming less universalistic and more specific. At the same time, the audience's basic orientation towards television begins to change. Everyday conversation changes from 'What did you think of that programme last night?' to an initial 'Did you see that programme last night?' or even 'I caught an interesting programme last night...'. This change is crucial. The first attitude is that of the era of scarcity, in which it was quite natural to assume that anyone would probably have seen the same programme as you. But in the era of availability, no such convenient assumption can be made. The audience has fragmented, and television programmes can no longer claim, as they could in the era of scarcity, that they were definitive, that their necessary role was to lay out all the facts of the case, or, if fiction, to consist of one complete story in every episode. Now audiences have choice, and no one programme can assume that it has the same level of social importance as its equivalent had in the era of scarcity. However, this does not mean that television itself has ceased to matter. It means only that any individual programme has to consider itself part of a larger process, the distinctive process of television in the era of availability, which I call 'working through'. This is television's new role in the era of multiplying consumer choice and escalating social difference and antagonism.

In this new context, television offers an important social forum in which the complexities and anxieties of difference explored by Gilroy and others can be explored. It now plays its part as one of the social institutions which try to reconcile the divisions that come with differences. Television in this sense lies alongside the public institutions of school, police and hospital which have a difficult role of mediation thrust upon them, and sometimes hardly know how to go about it. But television is distinct from these institutions in at least two respects. It promotes the consumerism of choice through its display of options and styles, playing a key role in developing the process of differentiation. As a consumer-oriented industry, television also worries constantly about its customers and their satisfactions, expensing large sums on the continuing process of audience research. Yet television does more than this. It also provides the experience of witness, giving modern citizens a sense of complicity with all kinds of events in their contemporary world. It displays both the opportunities and the downsides of contemporary consumer society. It shows the everyday conflicts of meaning and expectations. So television in the era of availability has developed beyond the role it played in the era of scarcity. Its programming no longer aims to be definitive; instead, it participates in a vast, inchoate process of working through. It shares this role with the press and other media, but with the crucial distinction that television introduces both the experience of witness and the mechanisms of fiction. This process will be examined in detail in the following chapters, both in terms of its typical visual and generic strategies, and in terms of its management through the little-studied process of television scheduling.

[1] See, for example, press interviews and columns of senior executives like David Elstein and David Docherty, or Cento Veljanovski, *Freedom in Broadcasting* (London: Institute of Economic Affairs, 1989).

[2] See Les Brown, 'The American networks' in Anthony Smith (ed), *Television: An International History* (Oxford: Oxford University Press, 1995), pp 282-4.

[3] Traducing the ideas of the historian Francis Fukayama in his *The End of History and the Last Man* (London: Hamilton, 1992).

[4] Robin Murray, 'Fordism and post-Fordism' and 'Benetton Britain' in Stuart Hall and Martin Jacques (eds), *New Times* (London: Lawrence & Wishart, 1989), pp 38-64.

[5] Charlotte Brunsdon, 'Satellite dishes and the landscapes of taste', *New Formations* 15 (1991), pp 23-42.

[6] Cited in *Broadcast*, 19 March 1999, p1, it is an unpublished document.

[7] The question of choice and brands is taken up again in the final chapter of this book.

[8] Paul Gilroy, *The Black Atlantic* (London: Verso, 1993), p 49.

[9] *Ibid.*, p 201.

[10] *Ibid.*, p 85.

[11] For an analysis of the many meanings and uneven distribution of power in particular instances of gender difference, see Rosalind Coward, *Sacred Cows* (London: HarperCollins, 1999).

[12] Homi K. Bhabha, *The Location of Culture* (London: Routledge, 1994), p 142, citing Ernest Gellner.

[13] This is a process which is condemned in rather unlikely places. *Variety*, 12 July 1993, carried an acute criticism by its editor, Peter Bart, of Universal's new shopping mall CityWalk, a make-believe city in the centre of the Universal lot, 'designed and conceived to be a crime-free upscale environment, largely for locals who wouldn't dream of walking in the "real" city.'

[14] Antonio Gramsci, *Letters From Prison* (London: Cape, 1975).

CHAPTER 6

WORKING THROUGH: TELEVISION IN THE AGE OF UNCERTAINTY

Television imbues the present moment with meanings. It offers multiple stories and frameworks of explanation which enable understanding and, in the very multiplicity of those frameworks, it enables its viewers to work through the major public and private concerns of their society. Television has a key role in the social process of working through because it exists alongside us, holding our hands. Bearing witness to the present, television is no more certain than we are what the future might bring. Its strength lies in the way that it shares the present moment with us. The very act of broadcast transmission itself creates a sense of instantaneous contact with the audience. The act of broadcast and the act of witness take place in the same instant, whether or not the events witnessed are taking place 'live', as Chapter 3 has demonstrated. Broadcasting also creates a sense of contact with other members of the dispersed audience, a sense that others, anonymous though they may be, are sharing the same moment. Broadcast television is present both in the here and now of the individual viewer and of the world that surrounds them: the regional or even national reach of broadcast signals.

Broadcasting unrolls in the present: this is its novelty as an aesthetic form, The particular power of soap operas is one facet of this process. Between each episode, the characters have lived the same amount of time as their audience. They live life along with us, but in what Jostein Gripsrud so accurately terms 'a parallel world'.[1] News constantly updates on different running stories, and each bulletin knows no more about the future than we do. Bulletins bring the audience up to date ('up to speed' in a term presumably borrowed from the technology of reel to reel videotape), but can only speculate about the future. Broadcast news exists in the same moment as its audience, and so it has no more certainty about the future than they do. Instead, it accompanies them through life, allowing each individual to define their personal present as part of a general phenomenon: the contemporary. This link between 'my' present with 'their' present and the present of 'others' lies behind many of the rituals of news-watching, catching the news nightly to confirm a sense of connectedness[2] which can assuage the feelings of complicity that is part of the process of witness.

News: The Present and Future Moment

The essence of the modern news bulletin lies in speculation about the future just as much as in witness of the common present. Each bulletin can only bring the latest fragment of a running story. News stories that are complete in one bulletin are almost by definition inconsequential: the domain of the legendary 'and finally...' items on Independent Television News in Britain. These are items which feature the weird and wonderful or the heart-warming, whose functions are similar to the local auto wrecks or the remote climatic disasters which seem to feature on news bulletins in the USA. Otherwise, news is a perpetual update. The act of witness, the evidence presented and the feeling of having a surrogate presence at newsworthy events, is fragmentary at best. It immediately gives rise to speculations about the next event in the story. This tendency has intensified in the era of live links to correspondents on the spot, who are questioned by newscasters anchored in the studio. 'What do you think is going to happen?' is the most frequently asked question, closely followed by 'Well, if that happens, what will be the consequences?' And it is a brave correspondent indeed who refuses to answer such questions on the grounds that they are mere speculation rather than hard news.

Television news is not simply about current events. It performs an important social function in trying to come to terms with the uncertainties of the future. The present is a precarious moment for everyone: everything in it is mortgaged in some way to an unknown future. In contemporary consumer-oriented society, this feeling is intensified. The world seems to be filled with potential futures, only one of which can ever be realized. To choose one programme is to miss all the others; to choose to go out to a restaurant is to miss all programmes. Time-shift recording is often used to overcome such quandaries of choice, resulting in the mounds of unwatched tapes familiar in many homes, or the more realistic attitude taken by those who say 'I'll let the machine watch that, then'. Every level of contemporary life seems to offer such choices, which will determine what kind of a future will come about. In societies offering more limited scope for choice, such uncertainties still existed. They were often dramatized in the genre of the 'marriage-choice' narrative, beloved of writers like Jane Austen and film-makers like Vincente Minnelli. Modern consumerism has intensified these possibilities, and made them part of everyday reality. Choice, and the uncertainty that haunts it, has come to pervade the present of its society.

In this context, it is only right that television news should concentrate on possible narrative developments. Each day the production of futures is speculated upon, and the speculations are proved right or wrong by events, which themselves lead to further speculations. Each item of news is always already part of a story. It has been predicted and space has been made for it. Through the mobilization of narrative speculation, the present moment falls into place as a moment in a larger process, known from its pasts and to a significant extent foreseeable in its possible futures. In the morning we hear so regularly 'The government today is expected to announce...' that we are no longer aware of hearing it. This is followed during the day and evening by 'Today the government announced...'. The rituals of lobbying, demonstrations and protests inaugurate new stories: 'Will they succeed?'. Murders bring detection, sometimes arrests and less often justice. In this world, a cataclysmic event is not a sudden natural disaster, like the eruption of a volcano or a flash flood. For the stage is already set for such events. They are part of an established news genre of disaster spectacles, and fit within overarching narratives of looming ecological catastrophe. As Paddy Scannell puts it:

> Broadcasting is always already ahead of itself. It is always already pro-jected beyond the day that we and it are in, and indeed it must be so in order to produce for us the day that we are in. In always-being-ahead-of-itself the futuricity of broadcasting shows up: that is, the future *is* always already someway somehow structured in advance, it is always anticipated (prepared for, cared for) in such structures.[3]

Cataclysmic events are of an entirely different order to natural disasters which happen randomly but are an expected part of the world. Cataclysmic events are those that short-circuit narrative expectations. One such was the death in a car accident of Diana, Princess of Wales in August 1997. Diana was a figure around whom a particularly dense set of narratives coalesced. She had been a figure of intense media speculation through her failed marriage with the Prince of Wales, her rumoured affairs, her conscious attempts to remake her image, and her uneasy relationships with the press. Indeed, at the moment of her sudden death, the press were again rewriting the Diana story. Positions were being taken on the pos-sibility of her marriage to Dodi Al Fayed, speculations were being made about whether she would be happy, and what such a marriage might mean for her tense relationship with the Royal Family. Many commentators (and there were always many) took an intensely moralistic line, and were indicating their hostility to the marriage which itself was still a matter of speculation. Indeed, in the largely unread Sunday papers on the day of the accident, there were several harshly hostile pieces which the writers would prefer to forget. The density of the narratives around Diana was such that the arbitrari-ness of her death suddenly forced people to realize that this had been a real flesh-and-blood individual, and not simply the complex character who had appeared in so many news scenarios. Much of the shock of her death was attributable to this fact: she had been as real as anyone else. Her story had been arbitrarily cut off, with no reason. Now there could be no fairy-tale ending that would reconcile the problems in her life. It was simply finished without being done, as most real lives are. So the process of mourning Diana enabled many individuals to acknowledge in public their hitherto private griefs. 'I cried for her, but I didn't cry when my brother died,' as one man put it. Diana had ceased to be a figure in the process of narrative working through, around whom many contemporary problems could coalesce, and had become one frail individual again.

This cataclysmic event cut short the normal processes of news. News should be understood in terms of story-telling and speculation about the future. But more often than not, the news story offers merely one possible narrative and framework of understanding from amongst all the others that are possible. Though news narrates, it does not conclude. Its narrative forms are used opportunistically, to anticipate the next development and perhaps the one after that, but no more. At moments of crisis television gives itself over to huge amounts of such speculation. The Gulf War of 1992 for instance provided very few actual television events: the cameras were deliberately kept away from the action by the military.[4] Instead, talk proliferated about possible activity and how to interpret the few clues that did emerge. All of this is born out of a frustration with narrative. Media and audience alike are desperate to know the end of the story, and not to have to wait for events to unfold at their own pace. From this frustration comes the welter of detail and the unstoppable flood of speculation. Most news stories are ongoing, like the Gulf War, rather than in a convenient form with a foreseeable ending. During the siege of Sarajevo and the battle for Kabul, there were no clear ends in sight. Neither are there for the fight against inflation or for global warming, however much we might wish for one. Speculation about these stories continues within the news media and especially on live television, but in more muted form. Immediately a possible end lurches into view, the pace and quantity of speculation increases. The story moves up the news agenda, not because it is in crisis, but because it promises a resolution. Television news is merely one moment in a far larger process of working through.

Witness and Working Through

Television can be seen as a vast mechanism for processing the material of the witnessed world into more narrativized, explained forms. The term 'working through' is drawn deliberately from psychoanalysis where it describes the process whereby material is continually worried over until it is exhausted. Freud, in coining the term, describes it as the boring part of the analytic process from the analyst's point of view.[5] The subject of the analysis has undergone a revelation, witnessed something in their psyche that had hitherto remained shrouded. For the analyst, positioned outside the emotional force of the revelation, this is enough. Indeed, the incident or meaning revealed may well have been pretty clear to the analyst already. But for the subject, it is another experience entirely. This new revelation lies behind all kinds of resistances, and so has to be integrated with existing understandings and feelings. Space has to be made; it has to be fitted in and so everything else has to be re-ordered as a result. So the subject keeps returning again and again to the same revelation, turning it over and over. Television finds itself in a similar position. It works over new material for its audiences as a necessary consequence of its position of witness. Television attempts definitions, tries out explanations, creates narratives, talks over, makes intelligible, tries to marginalize, harnesses speculation, tries to make fit, and, very occasionally, anathemizes.

So the process of working through is not a straightforward process that takes in hunks of meat at the news end, and parcels them out as sausages at the other. It is a far more multi-faceted and leaky process than that. At the same time as a news story breaks about a racially motivated murder, for example, there will already be various other kinds of programming dealing with the issue of race and racism in various ways. Characters in soap operas will be confronting prejudice; comedy programmes like *Goodness Gracious Me* will be lampooning reverse racism; documentaries will be examining particular issues; the black newsreader Trevor McDonald will be being voted the most trusted man in Britain; and Rory Bremner will be using him as material for a satire on the tendency for news to adopt the forms of entertainment television. Working through is a constant process of making and remaking meanings, and of exploring possibilities. It is an important process in an age that threatens to make us witness to too much information without providing us with enough explanation. Modern television does not, as it used to in the era of scarcity, provide any overall explanation, nor does it ignore or trivialize, as many have criticized it for doing. Television itself, just like its soap operas, comes to no conclusions. It renders familiar, integrates and provides a place for the difficult material that it brings to our witness. It exhausts an area of concern, smothering it in explanations from almost all and every angle. This process of non-totalizing speculation is a crucial activity in an information-rich environment. During this century, industrial society has embarked upon a course that provides us as its citizens with more and more information about events that have no direct bearing upon our own lives, yet have an emotional effect upon us simply by the fact of their representation and our consequent witness of them. The fact that the representation, on the news, is necessarily skimpy and inadequate, snatched from the living event, makes our role as witnesses all the more difficult. The events cannot be poignant because they are radically incomplete: they exist in almost the same moment as we do when we see them. They demand explanation, they incite curiosity, revulsion and the usually frustrated or passing desire for action. We need, in other words, to work them through. Hence the tactical use by news bulletins of narrative speculations. But these alone are not enough. We need to carry out the same kind of process of repression upon these representations that psychoanalysis describes: a process that does not eradicate them but places them elsewhere, which is necessary for civilized life to remain possible. After all, we have come a long way in a short time. Two centuries ago, our forebears in Europe were watching public hangings and enjoying them; nowadays we watch executions in Bosnia on television and experience very different emotions. We have effected a fundamental change in so doing; but we do not really understand the nature of that change. And we are only just beginning to know how to deal with these nightly spectacles of incomprehensible or inadmissable human behaviour. The twentieth century has provided us with far more knowledge than we need to have in order to function as citizens, even perhaps as fulfilled human beings. Television's process of working through is currently one of the principle ways of coming to terms with what we have witnessed.

Television's working through only has relevance to the problem of information overload and empathy fatigue if it is an open process. Each programme of discussion or analysis can reach its conclusion, or at least an ending of some kind; each presenter sums up, even if only to note the continuing nature of the controversy; each speaker encapsulates their view; but television as a system does not totalize. This is an open arena, where issues, questions or worries are paraded for a time, within slots that are regular. The programme will be recognisably the same, day after day, week after week, for its seasonal run. The issues and people fed through it will be diverse and changing. There is a balance between the familiar and stable (the show) and the unstable (the issues and the emotions around it). Broadcasting works through by multiplying the views on any topic that are fed through its voracious machine.

Uncertainty

To say that the process of working through is open-ended is not to assert the radical pluralism that writers like John Fiske have occasionally proposed. It is not, as he has done in one essay, to say that 'there is no text, there is no audience, there are only the processes of viewing that take place in front of the screen which constitute the object of study that I am proposing.'[6] I propose rather to establish the ground on which the encounter between audiences and television texts takes place, and, in addition, to establish what the television text might be, given that it cannot be identified with the pseudo-certainty with which we can say that 'a novel' or 'a film' is a finite text. I am simply asserting the primacy of uncertainty over certainty in the process by which television makes meaning. To put it another way, a certain ideological permissiveness exists at the level of everyday programme content. Despite the existence of regulatory guidelines on content, ordinary working practices and so on, television will use almost any socially circulating discourse. All and any ways of explaining society, psychology and human existence can be sucked into the maw of television. Indeed, as the wilder end of the American talk show spectrum demonstrates, the operating assumption seems to be that the weirder someone may be, the better programme material they will make. In that specific sense, television in the age of availability is not ideologically normative. However, as Chapter 9 demonstrates, there are still mechanisms of control within the television system. They exist at another level, in the balancing of genres and the creation of channel branding that is the business of scheduling.

Televisual working through seems to be a process of reconciliation based upon familiarity and repetition-in-difference. Certainly, the forms used by television do tend towards the certainty of closure: narrative forms which posit a resolution; explanatory forms that offer material that is graded and organized towards a particular

conclusion. But television itself as a form tends towards the opposite, towards uncertainty and openness.[7] This I believe to be television's distinctive contribution to the contemporary age: a relatively
safe area in which uncertainty can be entertained, and can be
entertaining. Certainty, after all, has its disadvantages in a complex
and changing world.[8]

Television's very use of narrative forms pushes them towards an
openness that in many other media would seem intolerable, or at
least inept. The narrative organization of soap operas is complex
because of the number of different narrative strands that are in play
in any one episode. The narrative organization of drama series
contains one or more strands that reach a conclusion within one
episode, but many more that recur in different ways over the life of
the series. The dilemmas of the central characters in a drama series
are resolved over the life of the series; the story-lines associated with
the week's incident or incidents are the ones which are generally
resolved within one episode. Hence the sense of ending is relatively
muted: both soap and series drama depend for their continued
audiences upon their success in conveying an impression that the life
of the central characters continues week on week. In documentaries,
too, the narrative may cover a coherent incident and may be structured to provide a sense of ending, but there is always more to be
said. The characters will continue their lives; the institution will
continue its constant adaptations to the demands of the world
outside. Within its stable formats and developing narrative structures, television also shows a marked degree of discontinuity.

Discontinuity is a social fact of television. It lies at the heart of
the way that television exists as a domestic medium rather than being
anything inherent in its technology.[9] Almost all television programmes on almost all channels will be broken up by adverts and
announcements, will be cut up into episodes and so on. Even those
rare channels like BBC1 and BBC2 in Britain that provide programmes with no breaks still tend to make their own programmes
according to this model (either for foreign markets or because the
aesthetic is pervasive), or buy a considerable amount of material
which was originally constructed to be so interrupted. This aesthetic
of discontinuity is mostly no more than an acknowledgement of the
discontinuous attention which domestic viewers tend to give to most
television. But it also acknowledges the realities of the era of availability. No-one can watch everything that is on television nowadays,
or even the entire content of one channel. Any completeness that

television might offer will always escape any one viewer. Television is therefore at once both continuous and incomplete. It is used by its audiences according to the pattern of their domestic lives, and their desires for what they think television has to offer. Television constantly offers; viewers take up the offer only when they feel like it. Audience studies as diverse as the positivist work of Peter Collett and the radical critiques of Ien Ang[10] have shown both the low levels of attention given to television, and the high degree to which individuals in specific circumstances find particular television material both intensely moving and useful for the conduct of their daily lives. The fragmented form of, and scattered attention given to, much of an episode of a soap opera can suddenly lurch into a moment of emotional intensity or pathos. A couple like Ricky and Bianca in the BBC's *EastEnders* can have constantly sniped at each other for several episodes, for no apparent dramatic purpose except that this is the nature of their relationship. Then they will suddenly be confronted by a life-changing decision like whether to abort a baby diagnosed with Down's Syndrome. There is a sudden shift into emotional intensity for the audience. Every word now counts, and all the previous audience attitudes of irritation or even condescension to this 'not very bright couple' (as one reviewer put it) become a feeling of utter absorption in their dilemma. Low levels of attention alternating with absorption, a combination of disdain and involvement, underlies television's social status as a mechanism for working through and exhausting society's preoccupations.

Most television has embraced this reality and has learned to base its work upon it. Television institutions around the world have intensified the medium's unique ability to source images of events happening almost in real time. News bulletins and entire news channels are able to bring these images and fragments of events into an initial interpretative structure that is inherently unstable, not least because the events shown in news bulletins are by turns radically inconclusive or catastrophic. Television then provides a wide range of forms which can, with varying degrees of co-presence with their audience, begin to work through the material that is brought in by the news, as well as to bring in different material that is specific to the modality of their genre.

Working Through and Post-Modernism

As working through is a relatively open process, a forum of con-
tending definitions with no final result, television has been seen by
many commentators as a 'post-modern' medium. The truth of this
depends rather more on the writers' definition of post-modernism
than it does on their definition of television. For post-modernism is
a term much abused intellectually and is fast becoming devalued as a
result. Zygmunt Bauman[11] offers one definition that is relevant here.
He sees contemporary society since the collapse of Communism as a
culture that has no alternative to itself. The certainties that went with
the divided world of the Cold War are no more. This also makes it a
culture that has everything except dreams; a society with no utopias.
Yet at the same time, it is a culture which promises that everything
will be available, everything can be obtained, all desires can find a
satisfaction in the market-place. In this definition, television is a post-
modernist medium because, seen as a process of working through, it
answers the fundamental problem that he identifies.

The result is a curious state of being. This is a society where
everything is permitted but nothing can find validation. This 'post-
modern' world is defined by the loss of the overarching ideals that
validated the modern era: the ideals of progress, of superior development, the motors of European expansion since the seventeenth
century. Postmodernist theory argues that no one explanation has
priority or ascendance over another. There can be no totalizing
explanation of events, and no theory that can project a grand
narrative into the future. The new millennium has already taken
shape. After three centuries of certainty, we have entered an era
where no certainties claim universal support. Specific beliefs are
adhered to, of course, but, in a myriad of ways, they have to take
into account their opposites, their outsides, their competitors and
their cohabitees. There are no 'mental horizons' any more, since
there are no universal certainties to form those horizons. Each belief
has its horizons, and each of its competitors can point them out.

Many theorists of post-modernism deduce from this that the
contemporary era is one in which there are no necessary beliefs, that
since nothing necessarily commands allegiance in society, then every
belief is contingent and thereby devalued. Since absolute beliefs are
intellectually unsustainable, it is deduced that relativism is the only
possible position to take. But this is to ignore the desire for, and

even necessity of, personal codes and beliefs. It conflates an intellectual position with the practice of everyday life: a common enough
mistake among intellectuals. For it is a different proposition to say
that any belief now has to take account of different beliefs that
surround it, jostle it and point out its areas of blindness and incon-
sistency. Beliefs nevertheless continue to be lived, and form a
necessary bedrock for individual existence. Bauman deduces from
this that cold tolerance is not enough between differing beliefs and the
lifestyles that accompany them.[12] What is needed is 'sympathy', and
sympathy is the product of television's process of working through. By
placing explanations, rearranging the facts, looking from all possible
angles, using the different emotional registers of its differing genres,
television is able to produce sympathy across the process of differentiation that is modern consumer society. This process never comes to
a definitive conclusion because none are available. It pushes the
multiplicity of explanation as far as it will go, making the strange seem
understandable, or at least acceptable. To that extent only, television in
the era of availability can be seen as a post-modern form.

The Limits of Working Through

Working through is a rough and ready process, the unwitting by-
product of the economic drive to expand television as part of a
general development of consumer choice. So it is not a universal
panacea for all social conflicts and all personal problems. Neither is
it a necessary part of modern broadcasting. With a considerable
degree of coercion and central control, television can still be brought
to heel and be bent to the will of particular governments. Within
more liberal democracies, however, television services seem to be
engaged in the general process of working through. Even here,
though, it has its limits. Where social antagonisms are really irreducible, television's contribution is often slight. It can provide some
variety of opinion and some accounts from unexpected angles. It can
provide stories – fictional or documentary – which dramatize the
complexities of the lives of particular individuals, pulling away from
the centripetal force of dominant preconceptions. In this way, the
irreducible antagonism becomes relatively familiar, part of the

texture of contemporary life, and to that limited degree it becomes slightly more acceptable.

Even then, to take a specific instance, British television has done relatively little to work through the puzzling phenomenon of Muslim fundamentalism. There is a cast of characters and stock of happenings that spring out of news events: the bomber; the Taliban; the burning of Salman Rushdie's book *The Satanic Verses*; the veiled women. Sometimes serious talk will tackle the question directly. But relatively little is done within the more indirect – and hence more necessary – arenas that television provides. Muslim fundamentalism is not a phenomenon that we can see from the inside, through the characters of soap opera or fiction. It does not appear as a dilemma for particular individuals, a genuine problem of choice between directions in life, something that perhaps provides certainty in an uncertain world. Nor, therefore, is it seen as a complicated phenomenon, with its own internal hesitations and uncertainties. It remains a thing, 'Muslim fundamentalism': out there, unified, mysterious and threatening. This is, at least up to the point of writing, a failure in the process of working through, which serves to highlight how important the process is elsewhere.

Public Service Broadcasting: A New Definition

The television industry itself has been slow to realize that its social role has changed along with its economic structure during the era of availability. Mesmerized perhaps by the notion of 'consumer choice',[13] notions of public service broadcasting have been slow to adapt to this new reality. Public service broadcasters throughout the 1980s were dominated by their inheritance from the era of scarcity. The provision of definitive programmes went hand in hand with a notion of providing a service that lived up to the ideals of a social improvers' agenda rather than those of a simple servant of the market forces. Yet to see television as a process of working through is to re-interpret the ideals of public service for a new era. The market-place accentuates social differences with the inevitable consequence of the intensification of social antagonisms. The role of a public service broadcaster in this new environment is to provide the space in which these antagonisms can be explored, but without appearing to explore them in any explicit way. No longer the agent of a standardizing notion of national unity, public service broadcasting can provide the forum within which the emerging culture of multiple identities can negotiate its antagonisms. This is in many ways the opposite of its former role: instead of providing displays of national unity, it deals in displays of national disunity, the better to bring about ways of resolving them. Instead of establishing a national form of standard speech, it increases the range of accents and forms of speech that can be universally understood.[14] The new public service broadcasting is no longer concerned with imposing consensus, but with working through new possibilities of consensus. It is concerned with exploring diversity rather than trying to divide social exchanges into the typical and the minority. The traditional strategies once used by organizations like the BBC no longer work. Low-budget slots for minority expression belong to a different era in broadcasting.

So how is public service television to make editorial decisions based on this new perspective? Market research with its particular objectives cannot provide the means by which a successful editorial policy can be launched. Television programmes and services are certainly the subject of consumer choices, but they are not consumed in the same way as a take-away pizza. Marketing can provide a useful orientation to the best placing of programmes to attract particular kinds of people, and it can of course drive the design and editorial choices of programmes about consumer choices: holidays, antiques, food and drink. But the complex commodities of entertainment rest on the satisfaction of demands arising more directly from the sources of social tension. Drama and entertainment derive their power from their displaced working through of current and perennial anxieties. In its new public service role television can return again and again in slightly differing ways to the same nagging social antagonisms. It can use all the genres of fiction and factual programming to do so. Narrative provides empathy with attitudes that are seen, through successive scenes, increasingly from the inside rather than the outside. Yet television is often at its best in this process when it does not confront social problems directly, and does not seek to articulate a particular position in a programmatic way. An example of the kind of television which fits this new definition of public service can be found among the surprise successes of the BBC in recent years: the comedy series *Absolutely Fabulous*. Here, finally, is a feminist sensibility expressed in a way that allows a broad range of people to enter into it without quite knowing what it is. The series was an unexpected success for BBC2, the minority channel, and was immediately transferred to BBC1. It is filled with the outrageous defiant humour of women who are profoundly unsure of their position in the world. It is the humour of the pre-emptive strike and no holds barred.

Absolutely Fabulous can be vaguely disconcerting for a man to watch: it provides both empathy and distance. It may well offend those who practise the difficult art of 'political correctness', if any such people exist outside the fevered imaginings of newspaper columnists and other such commentators.[15] It certainly seems to offend anyone with an over-developed sense of how things ought to be. In 1993, Melanie Phillips, then a columnist with the *Observer* newspaper known as a scourge of the 'political correctness' movement, condemned the series as anti-feminist. Her argument to the Royal Television Society Convention was that the humour was directed at the values of feminism, rather than at the ways that the characters deal with their problems. *Absolutely Fabulous* disturbs as it entertains. This is its importance in pointing to a new way of thinking about the role of public service broadcasting. The series lets us into the emotional complexes of its characters; it allows us to experience, within a situation comedy format, what women feel like in a public role, women aggressively uncertain about the nature of their identities. Viewed another way, of course, it is extraordinary that such a distinctive voice has taken so long to appear on British television, when it has been abroad in British society for at least twenty years. Perhaps it is another symptom of the way that public service broadcasting has been so demoralized by attacks upon it from within broadcasting that it has failed to notice the profound changes that have taken place in the public whom broadcasting is supposed to serve.

Working through is a characteristic of television's era of availability. It is a discursive activity, one that takes place across programming that, ostensibly, might seem to be about different things or something entirely trivial. Television's genres seize hold of any appropriate material, and the different emotional registers of television's generic structure are central to the process. Indeed, the generic mix of particular channels and particular broadcasting environments defines the character and effectiveness of the process of working through. The activity of scheduling defines the nature, range and quality of that generic mixture. Yet before examining some of television's major genres and their contribution to this process, a further dimension has to be explored. This chapter has tended to present television as a verbal medium only, concerned with ideas and speech. But this is no longer so, if it ever was. The visual dimension of television has undergone a revolution of its own in the era of availability. The process of working through has been crucially furthered by television's increasing visual sophistication, brought about by new technologies of image manipulation.

---

[1] Jostein Gripsrud, *The Dynasty Years: Hollywood Television and Critical Media Studies* (London: Routledge, 1995), p 250.

[2] This point is well made by Daniel Dayan and Elihu Katz in 'Performing media events' in Curran *et al* (eds), *Impacts and Influences: Essays on Media Power in the Twentieth Century* and in their book *Media Events: The Live Broadcasting of History* (Cambridge: Harvard University Press, 1992).

[3] Paddy Scannell, *Radio, Television and Modern Life: A Phenomenological Approach* (Oxford: Basil Blackwell, 1996), p 152.

[4] See David Morrison, *Television and the Gulf War* (London: John Libbey and Company Ltd, 1992).

[5] 'The doctor has nothing else to do than wait and let things take their course, a course which cannot be avoided nor always hastened. … This working-though of the resistances may in practice turn out to be an arduous task for the subject of the analysis and a trial of patience for the analyst. Nevertheless it is a part of the work which effects the greatest changes in the patient and which distinguishes analytic treatment from any kind of treatment by suggestion.' Sigmund Freud, 'Remembering, repeating and working-through' (1914) in *Standard Edition of the Complete Psychological Works*, vol XII, ed James Strachey (London: Hogarth Press, 1958), p 155.

[6] John Fiske, 'Moments of television: neither the text nor the audience' in *Remote Control: Television Audiences and Cultural Power* (London: Routledge, 1989), p 57. Fiske's work has been extensively criticized by, for example, Jostein Gripsrud, Ien Ang and Morley in *Screen* 32/1 (1991).

[7] This point is well made in a very suggestive article by John Caughie, 'Adorno's reproach: repetition, difference and television genre' in *Screen* 32/2 (Summer 1991).

[8] The connection between certainty, evil and death in the context of narrative and meaning is intriguingly made in an obituary tribute to the philosopher Ernest Gellner: 'I particularly remember a radio talk he gave: On Being Wrong. Its theme was an asymmetry which, because of mankind's partiality for certainty and finality over uncertainty, always gives an unfair advantage to the bad side of the antithesis. It is rather poignant that in this talk he gave this example: life with its ever-present possibility of death is essentially precarious, but with death one retains a stable and absolutely unprecarious state. The word death is, in Gilbert Ryle's sense, an "achievement word". He cited a Gorki story about a peasant whose longing for finality incited him to multiple murder. Gellner suggested that the theological idea of the ever-present possibility of grace may be a cunning attempt to deprive the devil of his advantage by making the state of sin equally precarious.' John Watkins, 'Ernest Gellner, a tribute', *Guardian*, 8 November 1995.

[9] Many studies and disparate schools of writing have noticed this fact: see Roger Silverstone, *Television and Everyday Life* (London: Routledge, 1994) for a summary.

[10] See Peter Collett and R. Lamb, *Watching People Watching Television* (London: Independent Broadcasting Authority, 1986) and Ien Ang, *Living Room Wars* (London: Routledge, 1996).

[11] See Zygmunt Bauman, *Postmodern Ethics* (Oxford: Basil Blackwell, 1993).

[12] *Ibid.*, pp 143-4, 217-22 and 148-68.

[13] See Stephen Pratten, 'Needs and wants: the case of broadcasting policy', *Media, Culture & Society* 20/3 (July 1998), pp 381-408.

[14] It seems that some broadcasters have already managed to perform this function, because of the peculiarly fraught linguistic circumstances in which they work. In Norway, the NRK has opted to give the linguistic nation a regular familiarity with all the diverse ways of speaking the national languages, thus promoting mutual intelligibility. Before the creation of S4C in Wales, northern and southern speakers of Welsh had difficulty in understanding each other. S4C did not try to create or impose a standard form of intelligible Welsh. Instead it has eased the problem by providing each regular familiarity with the other's dialect.

[15] See Robert Hughes, *The Culture of Complaint: The Fraying of America* (Oxford: Oxford University Press, 1993).

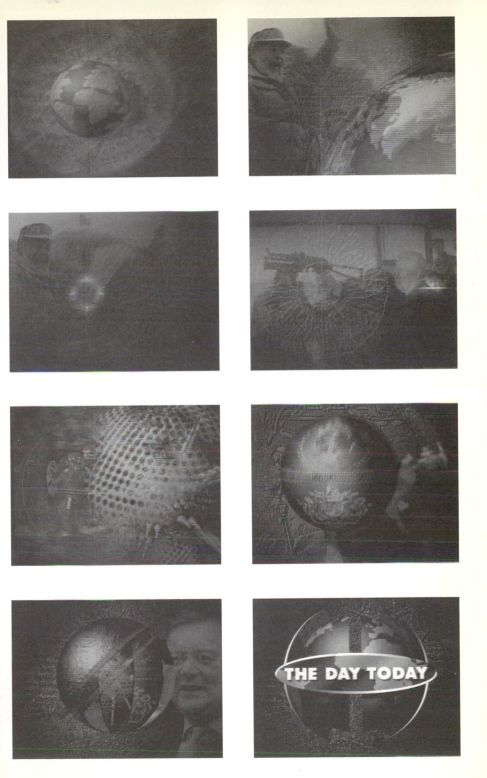

CHAPTER 7

WORKING THROUGH AND THE VIDEOGRAPHIC

Television's visual qualities have received little attention in critical writing. As recently as 1982, my book *Visible Fictions* could refer to the 'stripped down' quality of the televisual image.[1] But even as those words were written, a considerable change was taking place, one that has been charted in detail by John T. Caudwell in his trail-blazing book, *Televisuality*. Television in the era of availability has many more visual resources at its disposal than in the era of scarcity. They have been put to work in the process of working through. Television ceaselessly reprocesses the images of witness that it receives and creates. In the 1980s, television found a crucial new ally in its evolution as a forum for working through current concerns and contemporary meanings. It adapted the new technologies of digital image manipulation to the task. These allowed television to take advantage of the flat quality of its images, rather than to be hampered by it. Digital image technologies allow television to treat its images as pictures that can be manipulated in an electronic space, rather than as photographic images which reduplicate three-dimensional spaces. Television viewers are now familiar with images that spin towards them from, as it were, the back of the television screen, with titles and logos that appear to be emerging out of the screen. This is the small change of digital image manipulation, the ability to take television pictures and move them around within an artificial depth that can be conjured from the screen itself.

In this, television's use of the technology contrasts strongly with that of the cinema. Cinema uses digital image technologies to simulate realities and extend the range of its illusionism. The film industry has gleefully morphed characters ever since *Terminator 2*, and created entirely non-existent moving creatures in *Jurassic Park*, as well as adding the technologies to the existing arsenals of special effects to create ever more thrilling and convincing scenes of jeopardy. In film-making, the technologies of digital image manipulation and computer-generated effects are usually used in combination with other processes, like animatronics. The creators of these hybrid 'special effects' have become stars in their own right, and 'how they did it' has become one of the marketing pitches of mega-budget films. In cinema, these technologies are used for essentially illusionistic purposes. Nothing, apart from the passage of time and the expectations of audiences, separates them from Meliès' men on the moon or Frederic March's metamorphosis from Dr Jekyll to Mr Hyde in Rouben Mamoulian's film of 1932. Cinema remains a photographic medium, dedicated to the construction and reproduction of three-dimensional space upon a screen. Television has scarcely ventured down this track since the days when blue-screen shooting allowed the marriage of people in a studio with background footage from the image banks of the world. Instead, as John Caudwell has persuasively argued, it has taken its images in a different direction. Television uses images as the raw material for a process of work, transmuting, combining, changing and layering them in a way that can only be described as graphic. While cinema remains triumphantly photographic, television has found itself as a graphic medium.

Digital image technologies have, since their popularization in the industry at the beginning of the 1980s, treated the television image as a transmutable object. The pace of technological change has been fast, but the take-up of the techniques and their acceptance by audiences have been faster. For television had always harboured graphics in its everyday routines: television was a medium of writing as well as picture, far more than cinema. From the beginnings of television, it was felt necessary to identify speakers in order to place their utterances in a social context of class, power and knowledge. Chest captions gave names and social status, telling us that we were seeing and hearing the representatives of organizations or people speaking in their private capacity. The use of superimposed captions is such a long-established and unobtrusive television technique that it is hardly ever remarked upon in critical studies. Similarly, the limited vocabulary of the live mixing desk provides forms of dissolve between camera signals that could, if desired, be very prolonged indeed. So captions and image mixing, along with the use of graphics in advertising, all established fertile ground for audience acceptance of digital image manipulation. We are now used to ghostly slow-motion effects worked upon video footage that were out of reach until the beginning of the 1990s. We see step motion and think nothing of it. We take morphing in our stride when we see it on title sequences. We expect logos and cleverly formatted programme captions on even the cheapest of studio-based talk shows. We see images that mould themselves to the shape of a human face or body and do not bother to ask how much computing power went into making this possible. The change has been unnoticed and pervasive, as though it were already expected.

In the early 1980s, it became possible to manipulate television images – moving or still – as though they were objects in the black space of the television screen. Images could be wrapped around a globe or a tin can; they could be twisted, stretched and rotated. And the black space in which they moved could itself be filled with further image material. Two cliches emerged from the vast range of possibilities very quickly: the page turn and the shatter. Page turns took the place of cuts, wipes or dissolves. The corner of one shot was progressively peeled up to reveal the next. The image-shatter treated an image like a pane of glass which broke in all directions as though hit by an invisible hammer. Both techniques faded from over-use, but they had established both the acceptability and the usefulness of treating television images as malleable objects in space. Soon after, paintbox technologies also became widely available, allowing images to be rendered according to any kind of graphical treatment invented by fine and commercial art alike. Video images could become like crayoned sketches or like oil paintings. They could be smeared, posterized or given a watercolour wash. The appearance is of images worked over by hand. The screen becomes a sheet of paper (and texturing like expensive paper is often used) upon which video images are written or painted by the invisible hand of an artist. The electronic gives way to older, more culturally loaded, forms. Paintbox technologies also allowed the selection of particular parts of an image and cutting and pasting them into other images. This intervention inside the television image had previously been laborious in the extreme, involving the creation of masks through a vision mixer. Paintbox released the potential to cut out sections of action and faces from bodies; to insert figures within the planes of an illusionistic drawing; to intervene within the frame to release the iconic from the everyday clutter that surrounds it. These are techniques that can be applied to single images, still or moving. Other techniques have brought the simple art of captioning to an undreamed of sophistication. In the 1960s, chest captions were generated by positioning a painted board in front of a dedicated caption camera whose signal was superimposed on the video image, and end titles consisted of a strip of paper hand-wound in front of that same camera. On the whole, it was better to use film techniques for end titles. Then in the early 1970s came caption generators which could do the job electronically, and they developed ways of providing three-dimensionality to their writing. Lettering came with drop-shadows, and then with bevelled edges and embossing effects. Rather than appearing as though they were free-standing objects in the space of the television image, they had the effect of reducing that image to a written-upon surface.

This curious effect of electronic image combination became more pronounced as designers, editors, producers, directors and technicians began to explore the possibilities of combining transparent layers of video images. Once limited by the number of tape sources that could be input at any one time, the layering of images has taken on a new complexity since digital storage allowed a large number of images to be held simultaneously. Now multiple layers of imagery can be laid on top of each other in transparent layers, so that the furthest away can be seen through the nearer layers. Again, this does not necessarily create the impression of a three-dimensional space in which these images are 'hung', like the receding planes of a Disney animation of the 1940s (when this was literally the technique that was used). Instead, the effect is more conceptual than illusionistic. As Caudwell points out perceptively, 'transparent layering suggests a hierarchy of image levels relative to the distance the image components are to the viewer: deep layers seem farther; shallow ones seem closer. The tactic, then, creates a sense of depth less from illusionism than from aerial proximity and atmosphere.'[2] The key term here is 'hierarchy'. The images gain in importance the closer they are to the viewer. In the classic title sequence use of the layering effect, actions take place in the background layers, whilst in the foreground we see the close-up, emoting faces of the principal performers, whose names are superimposed in a custom-designed graphic style. The person and the emotion are the key elements, the ones we have come to experience. The situations are their trigger. Title sequences are just one example of the effect of layering images. News providers invested heavily in the new real-time digital image manipulation technologies in the mid-1980s, and news changed as a result of using their possibilities. The effects quickly spread out into other studio-based programmes and thence into factual programmes in general. The documentary form, as usual, tended to refuse the new techniques as a way of proving the authenticity of its images. Other factual programmes, like magazine programmes dealing with leisure interests and consumer subjects, leaped to exploit the techniques as soon as they were offered. Magazine programmes – a growing genre in the era of availability – now have custom-designed formats which package cheaply generated presenter-led material within a standard graphic format. They use the ability to combine images within one frame to make some move and others freeze or move in ultra-slow motion; to pick out successive details; to write caption material fluidly in synch with commentary; to use a huge range of print styles; to manipulate colour; to reduce depth and recreate it.

The distinguishing feature of the modern news editor, the state-of-the-art factual programme-maker and the successful magazine programme editor is their willingness to use such techniques, and their ability to render them unobtrusive. It is now easy to display simultaneous events together so that their concurrent, yet separate, nature is emphasised. Cause can be piled up on effect. Images can summarize a complex situation into an elegant sequence of graphi-cized images and writing. Whole situations can be encapsulated into

maps, diagrams, punning graphics and borrowed emblems. Graphic
television offers its fragments of images as in some way typical. The
frozen image of a refugee is treated to make a high-contrast background to a list of bullet points on the news; slow-motion bleached-
out images of holidaymakers provide a background for specific
images on the programme menu of a travel show. These are summarizing images, encapsulating experiences or ideas for a grazing
audience.

Such uses of graphics have become so commonplace that they
have triggered their own form of graphical satire. The BBC2 news
satire *The Day Today* in 1995 had its own devastatingly over-the-top
title sequence which absorbed many of the cliches of the form. The
titles were seen through a clear liquid surface across which pulsed
the grid-lines of a graph. Energy points of light ran down each axis,
and each time they met at the point of bisection of the vertical and
horizontal axes, a globe emerged which spun directly towards the
viewer before dissipating. Each globe matched graphically the
subject-matter of the background action. Each background consisted
of a brief iconic piece of news footage (Boris Yeltsin with a gun; a
dealer signalling from the stockmarket floor; riot police in action
etc). These were seen through a texturized surface in some way
associated with the image (banknote for stockmarket; crime statistics
for riot police; the green baize of a pool table for sport). Each globe
had a similar graphic match with the subject (coin for the stockmarket; spiked mace for riot police). The whole sequence had a sense of
excess of meaning, of heady overstatement within familiar forms,
and this was confirmed by the final segment in which globe after
globe wrapped over and around each other to a repeated final chord
of music. The point of this detailed and yet impressionistic description is not to recreate the sequence in the imagination of the reader
(though it may prompt a memory for some). It is rather to empha-
sise the sheer difficulty of communicating in writing the composition
and effect of contemporary television graphics. This is perhaps why
their status has been overlooked in much writing about television.

The Videographic as Interpretation

Caudwell writes, 'Television graphics have a built-in stylistic appetite for images. Because of this graphic appetite, images are transformed from the world of illusionistic realism into a frenetic world of spinning surfaces. Television is not just a succession of images or shots. It is a machine that consumes images within its own images.'[3] The question is what purpose does all of this serve, if any. Television has travelled a great distance since the beginning of the 1980s, when the emerging era of availability encountered the development of digital image manipulation. Both these developments, though the product of very different pressures, have combined to create the process of working through. Television's graphic processes take up images of witness and place them into relationship with each other. They are provided with frames and with written information. They are placed within a hierarchy within the single television screen, heaped on top of each other, placed beside each other. This is a working through of a purely visual nature. Digital image technology was taken up so enthusiastically by television news production because it serves to anchor the wild and the unexpected within a very explicit framework of understanding and speculation.[4] News graphics play an important role in organizing the incoherent world of news footage into the coherent world of news explanation. Wars become maps, the economy becomes graphs, crimes become diagrams, political argument becomes graphical conflict, government press releases become elegantly presented bullet points. It is all done with the aim of enhancing understanding; it helps communication by providing more redundancy, and provides emphasis by doubling information in both sound and image. Now instantaneity itself is packaged and interpreted. Television graphics produce the visual equivalent of the news-anchor's insistent 'What are the implications of this?', 'What will happen next?' News graphics enable television to carry on more effectively its activity of speculation, to cope with the impatience that comes with not knowing the end of a story, yet wanting it to come.

There is perhaps another reason for this activity as well. The process of working through can be seen as one of steadying the image, a process that was first suggested by Pierre Sorlin in a paper about the relative rarity of the close-up in cinema compared to its massive presence in television.[5] Television news, he suggested, brings in images that are barely visible and often inadequate. They are badly framed, wrongly lit, unstable, totally contingent. He then presented television's activity as a process of stabilization of that image material, carried out through documentary and soap, and ending with the near-cinematic visual quality and production values of television fiction. This idea provides one way of understanding the process of working through, as a series of partial attempts to steady the raw images of witness into forms which will try to integrate them into various kinds of larger picture. News is concerned with the images of its events that are as new as possible. All other criteria are secondary. So the quality of the footage is hardly relevant: news will accept poor quality images and poor quality speakers if the immediacy and the importance of the events will justify them. We are all used to the unaesthetic framings, the action caught half-way through by a sudden pan, the dubious quality of the sound, the electronic drop-out, the barely lit images, the images shot against bright light. This is wild footage from a wild world. News bulletins are constructed (with a great degree of uniformity the world over) from these hasty, contingent, poor quality images. The bulletins are held together by their direct antithesis: the controlled image of the news anchor-person (whose title here is surely significant), plus the highly contrived graphics that accompany the explanatory material provided by the anchor-person. News has pushed its image acquisition technology (that is, its cameras plus the means to communicate back to base), towards instantaneity. At the same time, it has developed the use of real-time graphics seemingly as a counter-weight, to try to anchor these vivid and unstable images of the near-present. Visually, news is an unresolved dialectic between these two extremes of disorder and control. 'Within minutes of origination in the Gulf War and the L.A. rebellion ... even the raw, amateur videotape footage was crunched into highly stylized videographic configurations. Scenes of reality, chaos, and suffering were immediately rendered as pictures, reflective surfaces and flying text-image projectiles.'[6] The graphics seek to contain the disorder of the world, but fail to do so adequately. Two antagonistic positions exist: the chaos of the world and the cosmetic solidity of the anchor and the graphic package. Television's process of working through will set to work to resolve the antagonism between these two poles, as they clearly constitute an inadequate way of perceiving the world.

It might be possible to define the degree to which the world beyond television has been processed by television by the pictorial qualities of the programmes in which it is worked through. Documentary images will have a more calculated sense of framing than does news footage; television fiction will be far more composed as a rule, except when it is consciously striving to imitate the roughness of news material, as with a series like *NYPD Blue*. But in reality, the process is much less even and logical than that. Indeed, television, as Caudwell points out, is full of overt visual styles.[7] Each genre has its 'look' (which is very helpful to the remote control browsers), and programmes frequently borrow the look of a different genre in order to mark off particular sequences or to give themselves a particular style, as *NYPD Blue* does in borrowing (and adapting) a news style. The look of amateur camcorder-generated material is frequently used to designate subjectivity. Other areas of television use the discernible differences between various image generation technologies to create a sense of style: this is particularly the case with material on MTV and similar channels. Television visual styles are overt, and in that context, much of its fiction has adopted the visual style of the feature film: the richness of colour, the complexity of the image and so on, which contrast strongly with the stripped-down images of the era of scarcity. But this is not to claim, as Caudwell tends to argue, that the increased production values and degree of overt visual stylization of much television fiction brings it closer to the cinema experience. It may do so visually, but that visual experience is more than outweighed by the narrative structures of television. Television drama and fiction do not tend to use the self-contained narratives that are typical of entertainment cinema. Television, typically, is an inconclusive form. Its narratives use the historic mode tactically and carefully. Its more habitual forms like the soap and the series drama are more open-ended. As the previous chapter explored, television refuses 'the advantages of certainty' in favour of the pleasure and pain of living in the uncertain present. Television, in this sense, acts as our forum for interpretations.

Digital image technology has at last given television the potential to use images to provide more than mere wallpaper (which is still a common technical term for images which accompany words without

adding any further meanings). The new graphic potential of television is being used to provide a myriad ways of summarizing ideas
and situations through images. It enables ideas and images to be
brought together into a containing frame which is defiantly not the
three-dimensional space which we identify with that of 'reality'.
Graphic space on television is a televisual space, containing yet not
totalizing, offering explanatory frameworks that are 'fit for the
purpose' but not definitive. The use of the videographic, as Caudwell
calls it, in this process still seems to make assumptions about the
level of audience attention to the image. Contrary to Caudwell, I see
no particular reason to abandon the force of the notion of 'glance'
that I put forward in *Visible Fictions*. This sought to characterize the
way that the aesthetics of television assumed a relatively low level of
audience attention, especially on the visual level. Television's new
graphic qualities still assume an audience whose attention is that of a
glance. It is perfectly true that television can be watched in a more
intent way, but its styles of visualization and narration do not assume
that it will necessarily be so used. It is also perfectly true, as Caudwell
says, that television has 'an obsession with making images that
spectacularize, dazzle, and elicit gazelike viewing'.[8] But this is over a
short period of concentrated activity. Graphics are used to summarize, and assemble within one frame or within a short sequence,
providing layers of information in one frame, compressing material
into a single but fractured space. They are designed to attract
attention and to provide an instant overview. They seem to suit a
glance-like mode of attention which is all that television can assume
of its audiences.

Graphic television is therefore the visual counterpart of the
largely verbal explanations that jostle for attention as television
processes the raw data of reality. Many would (and do) argue that
this makes TV somehow inherently 'post-modernist', that it simply
treats everything as a picture that can be stuck any old how in the
album that is the post-modern world: an album that has no end, no
index, no structure, no overall meaning and value. But the videographic consists of a constant placing of images in ever new relations. Equivalences are produced by putting two images of the same
size in one frame; a sense of hierarchy by placing two of different
sizes in one frame. The layering of images implies, depending on its
specific use, spatial relationships, a hierarchy, or a relationship based

on time. The videographic is not a post-modern soup of meaning. It is a crucial part of television's constant, even neurotic, attempt to place, classify, relate, give a semblance of order and generic meaning to the images that TV generates from the world and from itself. Graphics are another form of editing, of creating relations between material-in-images. This is the very opposite of a post-modern aesthetic, as it aches with the desire to create meaning and to measure one form of understanding against another. Rather the videographic is a working over, placing and processing of the witnessed fragments of the real. It is part of an explicit process of speculation, labelling, classification, reclassification, filing, placing and defining. It treats the televisual image as a manipulable object rather than as a picture of something. Through digital image manipulation, television has come of age as a visual medium. No longer tied to its mimetic base, it uses this base – the process of witness – as a springboard for ambitious yet routine graphic recombinations of meanings and frameworks of understanding. A crucial part of television's working through is undertaken in a purely visual way. Central to the creation of a new television environment, where working through has replaced the definitive statement, is the electronic recasting of the television image itself.

---

[1] John Ellis, *Visible Fictions: Cinema, Television, Video* (London: Routledge, 1982), pp 130-2.

[2] John T. Caudwell, *Televisuality: Style, Crisis and Authority in American Television* (Piscataway, New Jersey: Rutgers University Press, 1995), p 148.

[3] *Ibid.*, pp 147-8.

[4] Sport was the other area that drove the acquisition of this technology, and particularly the demand that it should have a 'real-time' application rather than waiting – as all other areas of programme-making were used to do – for the rendering of images to take place.

[5] See Pierre Sorlin, 'Television and the close-up: interference or correspondence' in Thomas Elsaesser and Kay Hoffmann (eds), *Cinema Futures: Cain, Abel or Cable?* (Amsterdam: University of Amsterdam Press, 1998).

[6] Caudwell: *Televisuality*, p 159.

[7] *Ibid.*, pp 3-31.

[8] *Ibid.*, p 158.

CHAPTER 8

WORKING THROUGH AND THE GENRES OF TELEVISION

O ne of the remarkable features of television is the way
that its genres are so explicit and instantly recognisable.
Channel surfers, idly pressing the buttons on their
remote controls, fleetingly glimpse all kinds of material,
yet they can instantly attribute accurately what they see to one of the
great genres of television: news, documentary, talk show, soap opera,
sitcom, comedy, drama or film. Yet at the same time, as John
Caughie has pointed out, these genres remain bewilderingly difficult
to define as they seem to encompass too many different kinds of
programme.[1] Television's explicit genres contrast strongly with the
reticent attitude of the Hollywood film industry, that great developer
of the generic system. Hollywood would hint at the generic placing
of a film through the title, stars and advertising material for a film.[2]
Television just comes straight out with the definition 'a natural
history documentary' or 'our newest comedy show'. One important
aspect of this generic explicitness is the way that television genres
can intermix and cross-fertilize in ways that audiences easily appreciate. Documentary and soap opera can create the real-life hybrid the

documentary-soap; talk show and comedy can combine in the shrewd parody that is the *Mrs Merton Show*.[3] Television's generic explicitness provides a degree of creative possibility.

Crucially, television's genres, known to all, provide stability in a system in which witnessed events of all kinds and their interpretation ceaselessly whirl around. The meanings change, but the formats remain largely the same. The generic mix of a particular television output is crucial in determining the nature of its process of working through. For each genre brings its own particular set of rules, its own favoured modes of understanding and interpretation. Each output may well have a breadth of ways of talking and explaining, of proffered forms of understanding. But each genre has its own particular emotional economy. So the balance between the generic forms in any one television system will give a particular bias to that system. It can be argued, for instance, that the concentration of American prime-time television on series drama to the exclusion of documentary, magazine programming and sketch comedy has produced the internal richness of its series drama. The multiple story lines and incidents associated with the work of David E. Kelley (like *Ally McBeal*) or Stephen Bochco (*L.A. Law*), perform many of the functions which are undertaken by these neglected genres in other television systems. So sudden outbursts of comedy or informational material tend to appear. But the overall emotional economy remains that of drama, involving empathy of a kind that sketch comedy like the BBC's *The Fast Show* does not. *The Fast Show's* sketches use comedy to celebrate eccentricity and simultaneously to show strong disapproval or even condemnation. Such a comedic moralism can only be a minor, incidental part of an American peak-time series like *E.R.* This question of generic balance is why the process of scheduling, examined in the next chapter, is so important. In determining the generic balance of each television channel, scheduling is a crucial determinant of the character of each market's television offering. This chapter tries to provide an account of television's main genres to show how their forms and emotional economies contribute to the process of working through.

News[4]

News and its narratives have already been dealt with in Chapter 6, and the distinctive quality of news footage and graphics in Chapter 7. News oscillates between images of extreme stability and instability: in this sense it presents an unresolved tension, and the work of television subsequently can be seen as a constant attempt to resolve that tension. News also defines a particular geography. It ranges the world (or at least the world it knows) in search of things that are happening now. News has two criteria: immediacy and importance. The relative importance of the events that news can cover is gauged by criteria of power and distance. The more that an event affects the structures of power in a particular society, the more prominence it may gain. The closer the event is to that society, the more coverage it may get. Neville Chamberlain's formula 'a faraway country of which we know little' summarizes how these criteria tend to work even today.[5] Of course, spectacular disasters in remote areas for which there is available footage tend to find their way into television news: they qualify because of the criteria of immediacy. Television news technology has been driven by the demand that it should provide ever more instantaneous material, to the extent that flexible digital video formats plus satellite technology are moving us towards an era of 'real time' news in which we can see events more or less as they happen. Part of television's process of working through is to deal with the material from the news in two linked ways. It uses words, providing forms of explanation and understanding, further information and the kinds of psychological perspectives that are impossible within the news format. Television also works through by providing increasing stability to the images of disorder: it reframes and focuses, it narrativizes and adds production values. The crisis of the news bulletin can occasionally become the made-for-TV movie. But in reality the process is more fragmentary and multi-layered than this. Usually, the process of working through is very diverse, involving talk, soap and documentary, and entails the introduction of fresh kinds of material to each genre.

Everyday Talk: The Talk Arena[6]

Television is pervaded with talk. Apart from the high-budget areas of drama production, the talking head still predominates, though it is increasingly processed by various forms of the videographic. Television talk ranges as widely as possible, often beginning as soon as a news story has broken. The first wave of talk about news comes from commentators in long-form news-based programmes like BBC2's *Newsnight* at 10.30pm, together with interested parties like politicians or the representatives of pressure groups. They provide immediate reactions and particular interpretations which serve simply to contain the raw events in some kind of temporary bandage of words. Daytime television the next morning provides spaces where discussion of issues or stories from the news can take place. Here the range of voices is far wider, and here begins the real process of working through. News events provide only one of the raw materials for this cascade of talk, as daytime talk shows look far wider than the headlines. They seize on any item of potential contemporary interest or outrage. Random bits of information, stories of personal experience, cries for help, all pass through the daytime television talk shows like *Kilroy* or *Trisha* in a relatively open and unstructured form, at least when compared to the news. This is talk: it tends to concentrate on personal experience and psychological explanations; in part, this is a response to the 'public' or official agenda of the news.

For talk is a large arena, encompassing *Newsnight* as well as *Kilroy*, *Oprah* and *Geraldo* and including even that arena of inarticulacy, *The Jerry Springer Show*. Through talk, the world of news begins to gain a psychological perspective, but many of its topics will not relate directly to the news. Especially in its daytime form, many talk topics are generated from entirely other agendas, those of the programmes themselves, or those set by the press, by the publicity machinery for people or products (especially books and television programmes) with a controversial message. This too adds diversity to the talk process. Talk lures in more of the world than the news bulletins of the previous few days, and in so doing it brings in a more personal, psychological perspective than news can ever provide. The talk arena is largely one of subjective reactions. It deals with problems of sex, of weight, of dealing with children, of tooth decay and bowel disorder, of make-up and romantic dilemmas. Differing explanations are offered, but not all with equal force. Some individuals act as more effective spokespeople than others; some programmes have agendas of their own. But the talk arena, though dominated by psychological explanations, is dense and conflictual. It provides a continual process of speculation on human behaviour and motives in the loose forms of everyday conversation. Everything that was in the news will pass through this process in some way or another: connections are made between discrete and separate news items. Stories from the news arena are misremembered and misinterpreted, bringing forward the subterranean preoccupations of individual speakers or of segments of the audience. This definition of talk, of course, is not confined to television: it is a fact of the whole audio-visual sphere, and encompasses the activity of newspaper columnists as well. Talk is a mobile form which provides, or attempts to provide, some of the narrative content and structure that the news cannot. Television talk presents speculation about the possible narratives that the events might follow. Television news begins the process with its constant musings on what may have happened; on what may be about to happen; on what would be the result if what may happen actually happens; and then on what could possibly happen as a result. All of this is bolstered by information about all the participating parties in the event, or participants who could enter into the narrative if events took a certain turn. The talk arena throws its net far wider in its search for frameworks of understanding. Talk is an open window upon the world, admitting anything that is of interest irrespective of its news value. So perennial social questions of delinquency, marital problems, self-image, working relationships, or psychological disorders of any kind are everyday talk material. In news, the politicians and people in the public eye hold court; in talk shows, ordinary people are brought forward for us to witness, showing their adequacies and inadequacies as material to be worked through. Talk is concerned with why: 'Why on earth do these people do what they do?', and this question is applied indiscriminately to the famous, the infamous and those who happen to have been picked by the programme's researchers. Everyone involved offers their attractive options and their little nuggets of information or experience. No-one has a privileged point of view, in the crucial sense that they cannot see into the future. This talk offers explanations of the present by the dozen and speculations about the future by the score, but it can offer no conclusions.

In the era of availability, different talk is seen as appropriate for different parts of the schedule. As television began to extend into the daytime in Britain, talk shows began to experiment with using the studio audience to debate issues (like ITV's *The Time The Place*) and to find people with no previous television experience to talk through a particular situation or set of emotions. Daytime talk evolved a form of conversation new to television, but already familiar from the radio phone-in: conversation of a mundane and spontaneous kind between people who had no special claim to be experts apart from their own experiences and their ability to talk about them together. This was distinctive and new, since during the peak times of the evening, chat still remained the domain of the celebrity. They are vaguely familiar figures, distinct from experts on a particular topic, whose views are nevertheless sought on a range of social issues that stops short of items of current political controversy. Many varieties of talk and chat programmes use celebrities. Some are entirely celebrity-based. Celebrities are brought onto shows by 'celebrity bookers' who are usually negotiating television's way through the thicket of agents and PR persons attempting to promote the celebrity or their current product. Celebrities are frequently people who are already television performers. The launch of a new television drama series is incomplete without the participation of one or more of its stars in the talk arena. There they discuss the thematic material of the series, the psychology of their particular character, and feelings or events in their own personal lives that have some resonance with the theme of the programme. This is not an 'incestuous' process so much as a necessary adjunct to television's process of working through since it provides yet another form of understanding.

The talk arena frequently vaunts its ability to deal with any and every subject. *The Jerry Springer Show* is precisely the point at which this boast is tested out: Jerry Springer's parades of unlikely stories of arcane behaviour not only test the limits of the talk agenda, they test the limits of talk itself. For many of his stage-managed (and often fictional) confrontations are liberally sprinkled with 'bleeps' where swearwords have been deleted. So the exchanges become totally incomprehensible even before the hoped-for violent confrontations begin. *The Jerry Springer Show* has a particular function in the crowded market-place of television talk: it pushes the genre to its limits and so ruthlessly reveals its inner dynamic. It plays with the limits of talk and explanation, providing a ritualized proof of what happens when talking can no longer contain conflict. It makes explicit the elements of staging that are hidden in most talk shows, and as a result has been frequently exposed for using entirely fictional encounters where nobody is who they are claiming to be. This testing of limits is an important function in any genre, and is particularly important in a genre like television talk which provides psychological perspectives which cross with news material and cross-fertilize with them.

Springer's celebration of inarticulacy and the staged violent confrontation had a particularly disruptive impact when it was imported into Britain. It pushed the agenda-setting of domestic programmes such as *Vanessa* on ITV away from the mundane and towards the extreme. In the words of one columnist:

> On television you can be insanely jealous or want to put items up your urethra, but you're not allowed really embarrassing passions like caring about the environment or third world debt. ... All they [the commissioning editors] want is the story about transvestite Siamese twins who steal each others' partners.[7]

This brought forward another submerged aspect of the talk arena: staging, performance and pretence. During February 1999, a sudden rush of newspaper stories exposed individuals who had appeared in numerous guises on daytime talk shows, and the relatively common practice of using theatrical and modelling agencies to find individuals willing to speak their real or pretended emotions. Fuelled also by the revelation of pretence in documentaries, the *Daily Mail* twice ran the front-page headline 'Can We Believe Anything We See on TV?'[8] Inside the issue of 12 February 1999 the story of 'two strippers who pretended to be sisters' was told alongside claims from modelling agencies that the talk shows 'are always on the phone to us' for performers. Elsewhere, the *Daily Mirror* detailed a string of cases where individuals had hoaxed the organizers of shows by playing roles for their own satisfaction: 'A male model Eddie Wheeler said he posed as an oversexed male, a Casanova and the victim of a female stalker', none of which he was.[9] The spectacularization of the talk agenda had brought out an exhibitionism that had hitherto been latent in the genre in Britain. It had also exposed the contract that such shows had had with their audience: that they reproduced the forms of ordinary conversation along with the sincerity with which most people feel they undertake their habitual exchanges. The element of pretence and performance had undermined that feeling, changing the nature of the talk arena from something mundane into a show. The widespread outcry, evidenced by both the long newspaper campaign and the reaction of the broadcasters, showed how deeply this betrayal was felt. The process of witness itself was compromised, as the emotional content of many daytime talk shows was regarded as being bogus. The television spectacle of talk needs a wide diversity of plausible experience and explanation in order to function. In the conditions of competition between television programmes, each will usually seek to differentiate itself from other programmes of a similar genre or in the same time-slot. Nevertheless, there are inherent limits in the system, and there are moments when a genre becomes formulaic or too narrowly concentrated, and begins to lose its appeal for its viewers. The case of the evolution of the genre in Britain in 1998 and the consequent loss of confidence in it, vividly demonstrates what happens when these limits are reached.

Soap Operas[10]

Talk mobilizes forms of understanding by having people explain and interrogate their reactions. Soap operas, current affairs and documentary are another, different, form of this working through. In contrast to talk, where psychological frameworks of understanding are tried out, these diverse forms employ narrative processes of understanding. Where talk, for example, speculates about the motives of destructive housebreakers and the feelings of their victims, the soap opera that incorporates such a narrative strand will show the event taking place in a particular context, involving individuals known to some extent to the audience. The event unrolls in the soap, in a narrative time that is not dissimilar to that of the audience's lived time. It can go in various directions: the housebreakers could be the offspring of other characters who need to be dealt with; they could be disruptive outsiders; their actions will cause a moral dilemma of some kind for the characters. We see the feelings of those familiar characters whose house is broken into and vandalized, but we also see the actions that they take and the consequences of their actions. Narrative supplies a structure of cause and effect that complicates the emotional perspectives that talk has begun to supply. More complexity results, and more contradictions.

Soaps in Britain are particularly adept at incorporating social issues of current public concern. Social issues, like my example of the vandalizing housebreakers, could be found in *Neighbours* or *Brookside* alike. By the standards of a Brazilian novella, it would be a very mundane, even marginal event. In each case, the story-line will have clear resonances with the constant public debates and official initiatives about crime, the decline of society and social disorder. In this sense, the soap opera works through news issues: not slavishly, item by item, issue by issue, but by providing narratives with resonance to the everyday experience or the prevalent thinking of its viewing publics. So the regional differences between soap operas, though real enough, do not affect the core of the genre, its reason for existence in the televisual world. Soaps narrativize, in the same time of experience as the lived time of the audience, the moral dilemmas in the lives of their characters. Soaps, as Jostein Gripsrud has defined them, exist in a parallel world to our own, one that feels very near and contemporary, yet which we can only visit through television.[11]

Soap operas multiply incidents around a core of characters that is itself in a state of continual but slow-burn change. Soaps themselves explicitly offer no final resolution. In Ramsay Street or Coronation Street there will always be another day, and the axing of a failing soap from the schedules produces some kind of catastrophe that destroys the community for ever. The power of the soap is that it appears that its characters are perpetually living in the same present as their audiences. The strength of this impression can be gauged when crossing national or regional boundaries and meeting people who are at a different stage in the development of the series. Soaps take the issues of the day that have been articulated elsewhere, particularly in the talk arena, and play them through their rich gallery of known characters. This is no longer articulation of personal feelings in the impersonal space of a studio. Instead, it is real individuals going through something for themselves. They are people whom we know, with flaws and strengths, who exist within a social framework of others whom we also know. Soaps are also identified with particular segments of the television audience. Much has been written about the predominance of women in the audience for many soaps, and they have been scanned for evidence of feminist tendencies just as Hollywood melodramas were before them.[12] Less has been written about the constituency that they find in teenagers and their importance, along with situation comedy, in the self-consciousness of families.[13] Soaps show how families work from the inside, offering a far wider range of insights than was available before television. *Neighbours* or *EastEnders* offer modern society's 'apprentice adults' with a wide range of narrativized dilemmas combined with a considerable degree of psychological speculation offered by other characters. Soaps therefore offer teenagers a privileged vehicle for gaining an understanding of human relations within a predominantly domestic and everyday context. It is possible to gain a degree of understanding through the slow-motion narrative resolutions of a soap. Whether this provides sufficient understanding to get through a real-life crisis is unlikely. The soap scenarios open up major emotional questions to scrutiny, that is all. Soaps do so through the combination of the empathy that accompanies narrative with a large degree of discussion of any situation by the whole range of the soap's characters. Such a combination is possible because of the regular and slow-moving nature of the form.

Leisure and Magazine Programmes[14]

The era of availability has seen the development of what had been a marginal genre of television into one of its central features. Magazine and leisure programmes with a degree of instructional interest were developed early in television's history as a means of combining entertainment with enlightenment. For the BBC, Barry Bucknell reconditioned a typical house of the 1920s for the taste of the late 1950s, covering panelled doors with plywood for that modern look. Forty years later, his successors instruct us in the art of recreating an authentic period look by undoing Bucknellizations. The 'makeover' remains the aim, whether the programme is *Ground Force* (where a team remodel a garden in the absence of one of its owners) or *Changing Rooms* (where neighbours make-over a room in each other's houses helped by a team of experts). But more has changed than fashions in interior decoration. The programmes now incorporate the homeowners themselves. The same evolution has overtaken cookery programmes. The incompetence of Fanny Craddock's sidekick (and husband) Johnny, complete with monocle, has evolved into the scenarios of *Can't Cook, Won't Cook* or *Ready Steady Cook*, where celebrities and ordinary people alike are issued with cooking challenges. Ordinary people have now come centre stage in leisure programmes, and their instructional nature has taken on a new twist. Instead of normative recommendations and an assumed 'average' lifestyle, they now present the astonishing diversity of popular taste. A considerable part of the popularity of such programmes in the early evening schedules lies in the casual insight they give into the minutiae of other people's lives.[15] This is more than what is usually termed 'voyeurism', however. It is an extended meditation on the nature of ordinariness and the mundane, and as such is important in maintaining television's sense of intimacy with the lives of its viewers. Magazine and leisure programmes offer instances of national identity at its most everyday and intimate. Their importance lies in this very pettiness. They sharpen awareness of all the subtle social distinctions that are conveyed by clothes, speech and lifestyle, and at the same time humanize them. They allow a small glimpse behind the designer labels and the style allegiances of public street culture, to see a more private side of consumerism, where commodities are infused with personal associations. In *Changing Rooms*, suggestions from the designers are often rejected on the grounds that 'we should leave that alone because I know that's important to her'. Leisure programmes show us an important process at work: the customization of consumerism to personal identity, that is, the construction of taste. In a consumer culture based on the exploitation of differences in the name of style, this customization and humanization are an important moment.

The leisure genre has also developed to explore the other side of this process: embarrassment. In programmes of home video footage like ITV's *You've Been Framed*, everyday mishaps are edited together for comic effect. Unlike leisure programmes about lifestyle, which are intensely national in their address, such compilations are traded internationally. Footage from Europe and America is spliced together with domestic footage of pets, babies, sport and cars. This is the basic form of a wide exploitation of embarrassment, where personal idiosyncrasies are held up for social scrutiny. Beyond the disasters-on-video programmes, this type of show is concerned with what is acceptable and what is not, and so is more intensely national or even regional in its appeal. There are many formats that involve the use of hidden cameras to expose unwitting subjects. Sometimes they are embedded in a wider variety show like the BBC1 early Saturday evening programme *Noel's House Party*; sometimes they can constitute an entire magazine of their own, like ITV's *Red Handed*. In this hidden camera material, children talk about the habits of their parents. Friends collude with the programme-makers to expose their acquaintances' bad sportsmanship or meanness in paying restaurant bills. Again at stake are the minutiae of personal mores, in a genre of programming that lies between the multiplication of categories that is talk, and the extended fictional narratives of soaps and the factual storytelling of documentary.

Leisure programmes, by their very popularity, produce their own undergrowth of press coverage, concerned with the problems of those who appear on them, whether it be an unacceptable home make-over; a victim of an embarrassing exposure who resorted to violence; or a prank that went horribly wrong. But generally leisure and magazine programmes are treated as a light genre, the televisual equivalent of practical jokes or workplace banter. So their overall effect is one of reducing the importance of 'being on television'. In the era of scarcity, a television appearance was an honour not lightly bestowed, and hardly ever refused. It carried with it the sense of privilege that goes with national recognition. But leisure programming with its huge appetite for ordinary people being ordinary has changed this. As Andy Warhol famously pointed out, everyone has their fifteen minutes of fame. If anything, the amount of time he surmised is over-generous by the standards of the era of availability. Warhol's insight is normally given a negative connotation, the sense that celebrity itself is inconsequential. Leisure programmes demonstrate the opposite: it is not so much that people are famous for fifteen minutes, but that they can be themselves – or, more usually, act out themselves – for fifteen minutes. The people who appear in leisure programmes have their own tastes and peculiarities and, at the same time, are 'nothing out of the ordinary'. This is a new delineation of the individual in society, a definition that has evolved within a consumer society that validates and exploits the diversity of taste. Taste is how individuals define themselves within the bewildering choices of contemporary society, and leisure programming works through this process.

Leisure programmes have developed in the space between talk and documentary. They have had a considerable impact on the traditional documentary forms. Documentary has a perpetual self-image as a threatened genre, which does not help in this context. Leisure programmes have downgraded the social importance of a television appearance, so the makers of documentaries are experiencing more difficulties in persuading people to appear in long-form

factually based programmes. And in most broadcasting systems
outside northern Europe they have eclipsed the documentary almost
completely. The generic mixture and social importance of those
broadcasting systems are poorer as a result. Britain has seen a
different development, a fresh generic mix. The 'documentary-soap'
has developed, for reasons that are discussed in the next chapter.
This highly popular form follows well defined characters within an
institution (a hotel, a store or shopping centre, a health farm or a
veterinary surgery) or takes them through a commonplace ordeal like
a driving test. This mix combines soap and leisure programming in
its insistence on engaging characters and its attention to the minutiae
and subtle distinctions of everyday life. But it also retains some of
the key characteristics of documentary, and indeed is stoutly defended by its makers against any accusation that its events are staged
or its characters distorted.[16]

Documentaries[17]

Documentaries on television have a peculiar status. They are a
protected species, yet, in Britain at least, they remain popular with
audiences on broadcast television. Elsewhere, though squeezed out
of the main broadcast channels, they are finding growing audiences
through more specialized cable or satellite channels. John Corner
demonstrates very effectively that documentaries retain an important
place within the public discourse of television, defining, implicitly if
not explicitly, a wide range of social problems and social attitudes.
Documentaries present us with material garnered from everyday life,
material which is distinctively different from that of both fiction and
news.[18] Britain has seen the development of a strong documentary
tradition which, some say, has been powered by a terroristic anthro-
pology practised upon the working class by the bourgeoisie, or by
those with substantial cultural capital upon those with meagre
cultural resources.[19] However, documentary remains distinct from
the 'reality shows' of American television by its insistence on
explanation rather than the simple confrontation of the audience
with the brute force of witness. Current criticism of the television
documentary in Britain focuses on three problems: the use of
reconstruction; the excessively intrusive activities of film-makers;

and the use of too many devices of narration.[20] Suffice it to say that such criticisms, though seemingly new, have recurred throughout the history of the genre. Documentary is based upon an epistemologically unstable foundation, so the genre is perpetually shifting to take account of its own impossibility. Documentary is based on a fallacy and exists as the result of a desire. This desire need not necessarily be answered by the documentary as we know it.[21] Documentary and the wider desire for factually based programming occupy a particular place within the universe of television. Documentaries provide material that shares some of its characteristics with news (particularly in the occasional technical deficiencies that come with reality filming), but offer the potential of a complete narrative, rather than news's 'today's fragment' of a story. Usually that narrative is one of someone not 'in the news': a historical figure or, for want of a better word, an 'ordinary' person. The place of documentaries has been altered by the rise of talk, which has provided a fresh and, to some extent, more equitable place for the display of ordinary people and their problems. The rise of talk and the demise of documentary have coincided in many broadcasting economies.

Documentary is defined partly by a number of refusals: it is not news, but neither is it simply fiction. Documentary distinguishes itself from fiction by refusing to use some of the devices of fiction, vaunting its relative lack of ability to shift viewpoint (which is nevertheless still considerable). Documentaries have a provisional feel to their camerawork, demonstrating that events have been caught as they happen rather than constructed for the camera, although, of course, such techniques can be imitated in fiction: witness *NYPD Blue*. Documentaries do not create an inner life for characters: what you see and hear is what you get, and what you have to judge. Fiction usually provides more signposts to motivation. Documentary also refuses to show some of the activities of its subjects (like, in Britain at least, their sex lives), activities which would be quite at home in a fiction about similar characters. Documentary, too, refuses some of the devices of narration, and some of the enterprise of the fiction narration. Documentaries have narratives (witness the slot designations *True Stories*, *Short Stories* on Channel 4 and *Storyville* on BBC2), but they do not have the narrative drive of fiction: there is more that is contingent, and less that is elegant. Documentary material is not organized, as a classic fiction tends to be, to deliver the ending of the narrative. Often incomplete or lacking in closure, documentaries explicitly aim to show how life is, rather than how stories are. This refusal, too, is one of the central ways in which documentary can distinguish itself from fiction. Such refusals are essentially tactical, defined in relation to what fiction is doing at any historical point. They constitute the ground upon which documentary works, and substantiate its claim to be depicting reality. The gamble is that documentary will appear more real because it is less fictional. Besides this series of refusals, documentary has other internal practices which are its own. John Corner has produced an elegant typology for the current sub-genres of documentary: the observational, the testimonial, the combinatory and the visually associative,[22] the last of which has fallen out of fashion in the era of availability. These types exist within a highly signalled genre: they are trailed, publicized and announced as 'documentary' in that over-eager way that television has of making sure that its audience knows what it is that they are about to get. Current affairs and documentary, to use the peculiar terms specific to British television, carry out a similar function of narrativization to that of the soap. Documentaries of the observational kind, to follow Corner's typology, set up a distinctive regime of attention. To watch an observational documentary is to see events unfolding which have not been staged specifically for the camera, though they may well have been incited by the camera's presence and certainly include a dimension of performance. Though the presence of filming is widely accepted now to have an ill defined influence upon the events being filmed, the situation itself has an existence independent of the filming. Often it is a public institution like a school, London Zoo, a Royal Navy ship, a National Health hospital; or a private institution like a family, a business or a psychotherapy session.

Observational documentary seems to allow access to real interactions, distinguishable both from the talk arena and the soap universe because the quality of performance differs. People in documentaries may be playing themselves, but it is themselves that they are playing, and sometimes not very well. Part of the interest of observational documentaries lies in the waywardness of their characters. The hesitancies of their real speech, the uncertainties of their actions and the inadequacies of their to-camera justifications of their behaviour provide space for speculation amongst viewers about their 'real' motives. Armed with the psychological knowledges which inform talk show debates and float around in soap operas, viewers of documentaries can bring their own analytic frameworks to bear upon the characters of documentary. Sometimes this has surprising results.

Paul Watson is one of the more innovatory of observational documentarists, and his careful casting of documentary subjects has created several situations in which these characters have attracted formal as well as informal speculation about their behaviour. Whether it be the dominant matriarchs of *The Family* in 1974 or *Sylvania Waters* in 1992 or the anachronistic toffs of *The Shooting Party*, Watson's characters have been surprised (and sometimes outraged) by the level of public debate that has taken place about their values and behaviours. Watson's use of the 'observation' technique has produced extreme results: speculation in the public sphere about the psychology of documentary characters which they as individuals find difficult to deal with. Such speculation exists, however, in a more muted form around many documentary characters.

Observational documentaries encourage speculation about character and motive within powerfully defined situations.[23] Observational film-making is fond of institutions because they provide context for actions and character. More clearly than talk or soap, documentary shows the precise social location of the people whose behaviours we witness. So observational documentary can bring us into the presence of extremes of deprivation and degradation. Yet however concretely the situation of the characters is painted, this does not necessarily imply a social criticism of those circumstances as in some way limiting or harming the people who find themselves in them. For instance, the observational documentary form was widely adopted by British television during the 1980s in slots like *Cutting Edge* on Channel 4 as a response to a hostile government: by showing sad people in desperate circumstances. It seemed that their plight needed no comment. All too often, however, the effect tended to be that of confirming either the hopelessness of the situation or the feckless nature of the characters. Explanation and comparison are the tools that documentary uses to remedy this problem within the open form of observational documentary. By assembling fragments of evidence from the world, from observations of actions to the testimonies of witnesses and the commentaries of experts, the combinatory documentary attempts to organize a coherent explanatory or investigative structure. Often, though, even with good casting of interviewees, the qualities of the real speech of these witnesses or experts tend to betray other perspectives. The waywardness of the viewing situation leaves the best organized combinatory documentary adrift on a sea of doubt and contingency. Its attempts at closure are not thwarted by this, but they can be compromised.

Comedy and Situation Comedy[24]

Television comedy, in Britain and Europe especially, seems to offer a throwback to an earlier phase of popular culture. Comedy shows take the form of disconnected sketches or 'turns' with lightning changes of mood, just like the variety theatre beloved of the clerks and working class of late nineteenth-century cities.[25] This kind of comedy breaks boundaries and flies in the face of convention and propriety. It relates to what some writers have seen as the carnivalesque and the festive.[26] It offers fresh definitions which are beyond the reach of television talk or documentary, elements of irreverence and satire. As Frank Muir put it, 'It is the duty of the comedy writer to probe the very limit of squalid bad taste.'[27] Television comedy also offers something more than this. Increasingly it is concerned with television's own forms of generic definition. Hence the string of news parodies from *Not the Nine O'Clock News* to the new aggression of Chris Morris's work in *The Day Today* and *Brass Eye*. More generally, a half-hour of sketches like *The Fast Show* provides a compendium of well observed television satires interleaved with a gallery of social 'types' whose roots lie both in the moralizing comedy of Charles Dickens and in the variety theatre. Television comedy thrives upon recognition, which is often slightly uncomfortable, of orders of discourse presented in disorder. This is an important role in television, but the fast changing format of sketch comedy is more typical of European television than of American network television. This is not to say that comedy is absent from the US networks, however, for television in the USA was responsible for the one decisive generic innovation that television has made: the situation comedy.

Lynn Spigel's book *Make Room for TV* provides a particularly perceptive account of the development of the situation comedy in America. The genre initially emerged as the solution to some of the internal problems of American television, but it consolidated itself because of its relevance to far wider social changes. The rapid expansion of broadcasting in the USA brought problems of finding sufficient programme content, and in the rush to fill hours, vaude-ville was particularly attractive. The problem was that it provided a sophisticated (or at least racy) city-based stage comedy and variety show. It presumed a male audience, and as television spread across the USA into more and more homes, its raucous sexual innuendo became a problem. So comedians were transposed into a more domestic, narrative context, and a new genre was invented: the situation comedy, where the situations were domestic, the comedies were of family life, and the characters existed in stable recognisable situations. But this genre was able to work through many of the anxieties of the new consumerist life of post-war America, of the growing suburbanization of the American cities, as it did later in Britain and Europe. Situation comedies showed how (not) to do it; they were comedies of the difficulties and unintentional hilarities of new domestic life. They showed the struggle with new kinds of domestic space and machinery (not least the television itself); the negotiation with new neighbours; the isolation of women and the frustration of their desires for an identity in the world; the separation of couples through commuting; even the emergence of bored youth and the teenager as social category.

This was the material of the first phase of situation comedies. Later developments took it into the realm of very different forms of humour, and into very different spaces. At first sight there is little to link *The Lucy Show* and *Blackadder* or *Fawlty Towers*, though the line from Lucy to Hank Hill is clear. But all are recognisably situation comedies, and they share formidable characteristics. They are almost always made for a thirty-minute slot. They feature a stable cast of characters and a regular set of locations. The core of the genre lies in its portrayal of characters locked into difficult relationships which they can only escape at the price of surrendering their identities. Often these relationships are familial (since this is the one relation-ship that no-one can escape), or relationships that closely resemble a family. So *Steptoe and Son*, *The Cosby Show* and *Roseanne* take place within families; *Hancock's Half Hour*, *Red Dwarf*, *The Rag Trade*, *Desmond's* and *The Brittas Empire* give us relationships that seem suspiciously close to the internecine struggles of families. Classically, every episode of a situation comedy begins at exactly the same place as all others. There is no cumulative memory, no character develop-ment. Each episode 'forgets' all previous ones, and each episode is a self-contained event. Perhaps under the pressure of increased competition, in the era of availability the genre has begun to adopt some measure of narrative progression. Some elements of slow-burn narrative development have begun to appear. In the American series *Friends*, the stormy relationship between Ross and Rachel has added a dimension of soap opera in an interesting example of generic interpenetration. Through sheer longevity the British series *Only Fools and Horses* began to develop the theme of Rodney's marriage, one which (unlike Ross and Rachel's relationship and its subsequent break-up) would eventually destroy the familial dynamic of the situation.

In general, though, situation comedy relies on conventions that were developed by such shows as *I Love Lucy* in the early 1950s. The genre took several years to develop in Britain: early examples of *Hancock's Half Hour* still show many of the characteristics of the sketch format, and include examples of Hancock's direct repartee with the audience.[28] However, as Peter Goddard has shown,[29] the series developed under pressure of competition from *The Lucy Show* on ITV into a full-blown situation comedy as the genre had been established in America. The genre has proved remarkably resilient through its short history, and has been adapted to suit many different registers of comedy, from the complacency of *Terry and June,* to the sly humour of *King of the Hill* and the corruscating animation of *South Park.* In many ways it is the ideal television genre: a stable format that can take on and work through virtually anything that comes its way.

Sport[30]

Sports events on television appear to offer clear-cut suspense narratives within a pre-defined time frame, yet sport also has some of the characteristics of news. Sports events take place in the wild world that news covers, but, unlike news, sport promises that the events it shows will yield a definite ending. Sport gains its key value on television from being live, from showing the audience an event as it happens. There is a peculiarly touching example of this value at work on British television. When the BBC intends to replay extended highlights of a particular football match after the news (the whole match having been shown on the subscription-only Sky TV service), the newsreader warns the audience that they are about to be told the result of the match whose highlights they are about to see. So after the words 'If you don't want to see the result, look away now', the evening's results are displayed in vision only. Sport, like news, depends on the suspense of not knowing how things will work out. Sporting events, like news events, take place in the same lived time as that of their audiences. But unlike news, sport guarantees that there will be a resolution and ending, within a clear and predetermined time frame. The televising of football has even intensified this tendency within the sport. As a result of pressure from broadcasters, important matches that are still at level score after extra time go to the infamous 'penalty shootout' rather than, as used to be the case, to a further replay game. Sport provides live narratives, full of conflict and uncertainty, yet with the certainty of an ending. Television sport, like television news, is a live form, and in this sense sport has an important role in television's aesthetic development by maintaining and renewing television's powerful impression of co-presence with its audience. Sport is a fascinating television form because it predetermines the time when the resolution will arrive, but no-one can possibly know what that resolution will be. Like a soap opera or a news story, the television sport event does not know its own ending. But unlike news or soap opera, it does know when the ending will take place: in the few seconds that it takes to run a race or the ninety minutes to two hours over which many team games are played.

Sport may be certain about when its resolutions will take place, but it still generates a sub-industry of sports talk and speculation. Even in the clear-cut narrative universe of sporting conflict, television still sees the need for an amount of working through. The result, the victory, is analysed. The relative performances of teams and individuals are assessed and reassessed. The dubious decisions of judges and referees are re-examined with all the electronic devices that television can provide. All of this serves to situate the sporting event within a continuum of sporting events. Other performances by the same teams or individuals are brought in as evidence that on this particular day, they were not giving of their best, or had found something extra. Then sports talk turns to the future: to the effects on the competitive league, or the national team, or the future of the particular athlete concerned. Sports coverage generates its own talk in an effort to dull the sharpness of the conflict that is a competitive sporting event. Sport on television provides a classic narrative resolution, a conflict with winners and losers, but television as a cultural form seems almost uncomfortable with the starkness of the result. Sports talk serves to knit the event back into the fabric of on-going existence by providing relativizing perspectives, and empha-sising the longer-term narratives in which the single event is but an incident. Television sport shows us much about the distinctive nature of television narration. The pleasure of watching sport on television lies in its special relation to narrative resolution. Sports events may not need the further narrativization that many other of our everyday or news-related concerns require if they are to be worked through. But sport is caught up in the same process. On television, its every event generates psychological and strategic speculations.

Fiction

Dramatic narratives on television offer a full working through of particular narrative options which have been foreshadowed in the talk arena. In the schedule alongside speculative talk, they offer full scenarios in which the audience can experience dilemmas from the inside. In dramatic narratives on television, empathy replaces speculative understanding; one narrative possibility is followed through rather than several being offered. Television offers many different narrative forms, each with their own attitude to narrative closure and the multiplication of incident rather than the ruthless push of plot. Single dramas, the mainstay of television drama in the era of scarcity, have disappeared almost totally as a form. Where they do appear, they tend to take the form of a cinema film, with a tightly organized plot and a strong resolution. However, the made-for-TV movie has an inferior cultural reputation in relation to the cinema film. This is not simply because the TV movie has an inferior budgetary level, it is more because it functions as a distinct form. The TV movie provides a form in which social issues can be worked through explicitly, often in the form of dramas based on real life stories. The *Movie of the Week* form on American television plays exactly this role, dealing easily with issues such as rape, AIDS, paederasty, petty crime, senility and so on, issues which the Holly-wood feature film industry finds it almost impossible to address within its entertainment formats. The difference lies in the fact that the TV movie is made for television, and so is part of a culture of working through.

In some television cultures, like Britain's, the made-for-TV movie forms a substantial part of what passes for a national cinema. There is a deliberate blurring of the categories as a result, so the role as dramatic forum for working through is carried by short serial drama. This form consists of three, four or five episodes of about an hour's length, with strong characters and a final narrative resolution, often the death of a central character which would preclude the return of the story as a format. This form is as much the domain of the writer as the director, and the writer often has central billing as the creator of the serial. The short serial drama was the form adopted by Dennis Potter (*The Singing Detective*, *Blackeyes* etc) when the single drama began to disappear at the end of the era of scarcity. Many other 'name' writers have followed as the form has an obvious attraction for creative individuals. But even at this length, television's tendency towards the discursive and the picaresque begins to assert itself. At three hours or more of duration, in a form broken into episodes, there is time for sub-plots to develop, for incidental characters to take on a life of their own, and for the dramatic intensity of the clash of single characters to give way to the dramatic complexities of ensemble work.

Beyond the serial (in length at least) lies series drama. This functions a little like a discontinuous soap, in that its characters can return for a further series, even though the main themes of the series narrative do achieve resolution at the end of the four, six, ten, or twenty episodes of the series. Often series are based in an institution which provides a handy flow of individual incidents around and through which the core characters live their particular problems. Hospitals and police have been staple television institutions, hence the trade term 'precinct drama'. BBC1's highly popular Saturday night series *Casualty* offers a stark and effective example in which accident victims parade their particular problems through the Casualty Unit and disappear at the end of the episode, never to be seen again, and often with their stories left hanging unresolved. *Casualty*'s strength lies in its ability to include short narratives which show how the accident came about. American series like *E.R.* or *St. Elsewhere* do not; their focus is entirely within the hospital, but this allows the series to have patients whose stories recur over episodes, even appearing sporadically throughout the run of series. In both cases, the central (medical) characters and perhaps the fate of the hospital itself, provide the overarching dilemmas which are resolved by the end of the series run.

However, American prime-time drama, which is widely exported, has developed a distinctive multi-stranded approach, especially in the productions associated with David E. Kelley and Steven Bochco. Series like *Hill Street Blues*, *NYPD Blue* and *E.R.* offer a large cast of characters and an equally large range of storylines. In the space of one episode, perhaps five stories will be significantly advanced. One story will begin and end within the episode. Others will continue through the whole season, or at least over a number of episodes. Other incidents will often occur along the way, such that it is often impossible at the beginning of any episode to tell what will develop as a major strand and what rest as a simple incident. Often comic or even parodic material is inserted amongst the serious stories. This is drama that is trying to carry the world upon its shoulders. It tries to do the work of genres like sketch comedy that are largely absent from prime-time television in the USA. As a result, this is a fascinating new development in television drama. And its attempt to contain the multiplicity of the world proves the need for television to work through the anxieties and the uncertainties of that world, and to provide the audience with as many means of understanding as possible. The European television serial is a more tightly knit narrative that does not have its eye upon its own return. Television economics, the levels of finance needed to sustain such production, dictate that the serial is more a feature of European television than American. The serial aims to resolve its narrative dilemmas within its limited run of episodes, and that resolution can encompass a dissolution of the core of the narrative. The main character can be killed; the central couple divorce; the warring parties resolve their differences and so offer meagre opportunities for further dramatic conflict. Even so, the television serial multiplies incident and marginal characters in a way that marks it as distinct from the cinema's more ruthlessly direct modes of telling a story.

Television narratives in general have a contingent and co-present quality about them: they offer themselves as narratives that are evolving. In this, television narratives are distinct from more classical forms found in novels or the cinema which are constructed retrospectively, in the sense that they are organized to reach an ending which is known in advance. Film-making for the cinema will signal in advance the fate of its characters. An extreme case is James Cameron's *Titanic*, which took an already-known event and intensified the sense of narrative predestination by its flashback structure which established that Kate Winslett's character was among the survivors. This did not harm the film as spectacle, or as narrative. Cinema has developed a historic mode of narration in which actions and themes are tightly organized in a pattern of crisis, innovation and repetition that is orchestrated to a particular resolution. In the classical narrative, everything is there to move towards (or to delay the move towards) a resolution, which the narrative itself (but not the reader, necessarily) knows in advance. So strong is this model that any extraneous matter, any digression, tends to find itself interpreted in some way as a contribution to this onward move-ment.[31] Of course television both transmits and makes stories that conform to this model. A significant amount of television output consists of cinema films whose mode of narration is overwhelmingly in the historic mode. Television equally makes single fictions which conform to this mode, be they made-for-TV movies or various kinds of single episode or short run dramas. Yet even here, the ruthless search for the narrative tensions that leads Hollywood scriptwriting to refashion real-life stories is less of an imperative for the American made-for-TV movie.

In Conclusion

In the era of availability, television's major genres evolved a process of working through. This is carried on centrally through the more mundane of television's genres rather than those which gather critical attention and professional plaudits alike. There is very little prestige television compared to the hours devoted to talk or leisure programmes, and television's real social importance lies within those forms. The future of public service broadcasting depends on the process of working through, on the continuing provision of wide varieties of viewpoint and lifestyle witnessed across a wide range of entertaining genres. Television is a forum, though perhaps not in the way that Horace Newcomb originally defined it.[32] Viewed from within, it is a chaotic forum, but in each broadcasting environment it has a definite shape, and hence definite limits and overall tendencies. Television tends to favour the psychological over the structural, or the personal over the political, to use an old distinction. Television is bound by rules which ban particular points of view. Television is pushed by the demand that it should entertain. It is pulled by the competition for audiences into any amount of trivia and sensationalism. But all these tendencies, whilst forming and limiting television's potential as a forum, also enable it to work through for its overwhelmingly domestic audience the enormity of a world full of information. Television's explicit and flexible generic organization allows it to spread as wide as possible, and to provide many emotional points of contact with the ideas and lifestyles, problems and opportunities, that it is working through.

---

[1] John Caughie, 'Adorno's reproach: repetition, difference and television genre', *Screen* 32/2 (Summer 1991).

[2] For cinema's attitude to genre, see Steve Neale, *Genre* (London: British Film Institute, 1980).

[3] *The Mrs Merton Show* for BBC featured the comedian Caroline Aherne who adopted the persona of a down-to-earth middle-aged Northern woman running a talk show with real celebrities as guests. In her fictional role, she was able to ask the kinds of questions that no 'real' talk show host would feel able to ask, and she was further empowered by the presence of a studio audience of older people with attitude.

[4] For another perspective on news, see I. Gaber, 'Television and political coverage' in Christine Geraghty and David Lusted (eds), *The Television Studies Book* (London: Edward Arnold, 1998), pp 264-74; Peter Dahlgren and Colin Sparks (eds), *Communication and Citizenship* (London: Routledge, 1991).

[5] See Klaus Bruhn Jensen, 'Knowledge as received: a project on audience uses of television news in world cultures', in Jostein Gripsrud (ed), *Television and Common Knowledge* (London: Routledge, 1999).

[6] For other approaches to the genre, see Joan Shattuc, *The Talking Cure* (London: Routledge, 1997); Mimi White, *Tele-Advising* (Chapel Hill: University of North Carolina Press, 1992); Joan Shattuc, '"Go Rikki": politics, perversion and pleasure in the 1990s' in Geraghty and Lusted: *The Television Studies Book*; Sonia M. Livingstone and Peter K. Lunt, *Mass Consumption and Personal Identity* (Buckingham: Open University Press, 1992); Paddy Scannell, *Radio, Television and Modern Life: A Phenomenological Approach* (Oxford: Basil Blackwell, 1996); C. Squire, 'Empowering women? The *Oprah Winfrey Show*' in Charlotte Brunsdon, Juliet D'Acci and Lynn Spigel, *Feminist Television Criticism: A Reader* (Oxford: Oxford University Press, 1997).

[7] Ros Coward, *Guardian*, 16 February 1999, p 19.

[8] 5 February and again on 12 February 1999.

[9] 12 February 1999, p 3.

[10] Soap opera has been much discussed by academic writers: see, for example, Jostein Gripsrud, *The Dynasty Years: Hollywood Television and Critical Media Studies* (London: Routledge, 1995); Tania Modleski, 'The search for tomorrow in today's soap operas' in Brunsdon, D'Acci and Spigel: *Feminist Television Criticism;* Mary Cassata and T. Skill (eds) *Life on Daytime Television: Tuning-In American Serial Drama* (Norwood, New Jersey: Ablex Publishing Corporation, 1983); Christine Geraghty,

Women and Soap Opera: A Study of Prime Time Soaps (Cambridge: Polity Press, 1991); Ien Ang, *Watching Dallas: Soap Opera and the Melodramatic Imagination* (London: Methuen, 1985); Robert C. Allen, *Speaking of Soap Operas* (Chapel Hill and London: University of North Carolina Press, 1985); Robert C. Allen (ed), *To Be Continued: Soap Operas Around the World* (London: Routledge, 1995).

[11] Gripsrud: *The Dynasty Years*, p 250.

[12] See Ien Ang, *Living Room Wars* (London: Routledge, 1996) and Gripsrud: *The Dynasty Years*, pp 163-98.

[13] However, see Roger Silverstone, *Television and Everyday Life* (London: Routledge, 1994), chapter 2, for a summary of studies which do open up this perspective.

[14] This relatively new genre of programming has been little discussed, but see N. Strange, 'Perform, educate, entertain: ingredients of the cookery programme genre' and David Lusted, 'The popular culture debate and light entertainment on television', both in Geraghty and Lusted: *The Television Studies Book*; Gary Whannel, 'Winner takes all: competition' in Andrew Goodwin and Gary Whannel (eds), *Understanding Television* (London: Routledge, 1990); Dominic Strinati and S. Wagg, *Come on Down: Popular Media Culture in Postwar Britain* (London: Routledge, 1992).

[15] *Ground Force*, a BBC1 leisure series in which a family garden is remodelled in the absence of a family member in order to 'surprise' them, has occasionally gained audiences of soap opera dimensions, with a rating of 10.42 million on 24 September 1998.

[16] The BBC1 series on traffic wardens, *Clampers* (1997), was accused in several press reports of casting as its central character an employee of the service named Ray whose job was that of an office-based supervisor. His evident glee at clamping cars was a major confirmation of the public image of this unpopular profession. The programme-makers defended their choice by saying that Ray's role as supervisor included going 'on the streets' at any time of staff shortage, which occurred regularly.

[17] Recent approaches to documentary include John Corner, *The Art of Record: A Critical Introduction to Documentary* (Manchester; University of Manchester Press, 1996); Brian Winston, *Claiming the Real: The Documentary Film Revisited* (London: British Film Institute, 1995); Bill Nichols, *Blurred Boundaries* (Bloomington: Indiana University Press, 1994); Michael Renov (ed), *Theorising Documentary* (London: Routledge, 1993); Peter Keighron, 'Video diaries: what's up doc?', *Sight and Sound* 3/10 (October 1998), pp 24-5; P. Humm, 'Real TV: camcorders, access and authenticity' in Geraghty and Lusted: *The Television Studies Book*.

[18] See Corner: *The Art of Record*.

[19] This definition was put to me by John Samson, pioneer of agitational programmes like *Free For All* and *Speak Out*.

[20] Documentaries are subject to regular scrutiny in the press, both popular and broadsheet, and these are the main concerns expressed in such reports. For instance, the *Daily Mail*'s front-page main headline on 5 February 1999 reported: 'A gritty prime-time Channel 4 documentary contained faked scenes, it was admitted last night. The confession that viewers had been duped yet again came only weeks after the Independent Television Commission fined Carlton a record £2 million after key sections in an award-winning drugs 'expose' [*The Connection*] were proved bogus ... Channel 4 is already 'on probation' over staged film in the *Cutting Edge* documentary *Rogue Males* last February. It could now face a hefty fine from the ITC which is to

investigate *Too Much Too Young: Chickens*, a programme about rent boys on the streets of Glasgow screened two weeks ago.' Channel 4 was eventually fined £150,000 for this infringement of the ITC regulations governing factual programming.

[21] See Nichols: *Blurred Boundaries*.

[22] See Corner: *The Art of Record*.

[23] An example of such speculation is the *Guardian* article, 'Eat, drink, be bigoted, tomorrow we vote' about Watson's *Dinner Party* that gathered eight Conservative voters together to voice their views around a dinner table (13 March 1997, p 3). A report followed on 15 March: 'Yesterday their decision to take part was looking a bit of a mistake. Even the *Daily Telegraph* [a right wing paper] described their views as bigoted. What to do? After breakfast and a restorative brandy, Bill, Henry and George repaired to George's pub to drown their sorrows. "The other five are devastated. They don't want to know about it," said George. "We are reasonably intelligent people – we are deep thinking people. The way it has been portrayed is that we are a shallow lot of public school shits." … A spokesman for Granada, which made the 50 minute *Cutting Edge* documentary, denied the eight had been "stitched up". "They have not seen the film yet" she added.' *Guardian*, 15 March 1997, p 5.

[24] Discussions of situation comedy include P. Kirkham and B. Skeggs, '*Absolutely Fabulous*: absolutely feminist' in Geraghty and Lusted: *The Television Studies Book*; Steve Neale and Frank Krutnik, *Popular Film and Television Comedy* (London: Routledge, 1990); David Marc, *Demographic Vistas: TV in American Culture* (Philadelphia: University of Pennsylvania Press, 1996); Patricia Mellencamp, 'Situation comedy, feminism, and Freud: discourses of Gracie and Lucy' and K. Rowe, 'Roseanne: unruly woman as domestic goddess', both in Brunsdon, D'Acci and Spigel: *Feminist Television*; D. Grote, *The End of Comedy: The Sitcom and the Comedic Tradition* (Hamden, Connecticut: Shoe String Press, 1983); Stephen Jhally and Justin Lewis, *Enlightened Racism: The Cosby Show, Audiences, and the Myth of the American Dream* (Boulder, Colorado: Westview Press, 1992).

[25] Neale and Krutnik: *Popular Film*.

[26] See Mikhael Bakhtin, *The Bakhtin Reader* (London: Edward Arnold, 1994).

[27] Frank Muir, *A Kentish Lad* (London: Corgi, 1999).

[28] See for example the episode from 9 December 1957, from the third series which was broadcast live. At one point Hancock fluffs a line and remarks to camera 'I'll take a run at it …'. During the same scene he reacts with an aside to an unexpected laugh from the audience. The second scene is a routine with a postman and policeman (Dick Emery and Derek Guyler respectively) which could have come straight from a variety show, complete with funny voices and visual comedy.

[29] Peter Goddard, 'Hancock's Half Hour: a watershed in British television comedy' in John Corner (ed), *Popular Television in Britain: Studies in Cultural History* (London: British Film Institute, 1991).

[30] Sport receives too little coverage in serious discussions of television. Frances Wheen's *Television* (London, Century, 1985), derived from the definitive Granada TV series of 1985, gives sport its rightful place as one of the great forces for technological and aesthetic innovation in television. Other discussions include T. O'Neil, *The Game Behind the Game: High Pressure, High Stakes in Television Sports* (New York: Harper & Row, 1989); R. Powers, *Supertube: The Rise of Television Sports* (New York: Conrad-

McCann, 1984); Gary Whannel, *Fields in Vision: Television Sport and Cultural Transformation* (London: Routledge, 1992).

[31] See David Bordwell, *Narration in the Fiction Film* (London: Methuen, 1985).

[32] See Horace Newcomb, *Television: The Most Popular Art* (New York: Anchor Books, 1974).

CHAPTER 9

SCHEDULING: WHERE POWER LIES IN TELEVISION

Television's working through is nowhere a neutral social process. It is immediately evident that specific channels and specific national broadcasting systems have wildly different generic mixes. Some genres are heavily featured, others are virtually absent. Genres have increasing or waning popularity; cross-generic programming constantly develops. This economy of genres is crucial to the nature and quality of the process of working through undertaken by a television system in any specific context. It is easier for outsiders to perceive the national characteristics of any television 'ecology' or system. But to insiders, the population to whom they are addressed, they appear to be a natural part of the tissue of everyday life. Every viewer inside such a system has another set of discriminations, which are correspondingly difficult for the external observer to see, between the specific characters of various channels and even of different time slots within the schedule.[1] Television itself is always specific, however much it may be amenable to generalizations. In every television system, national or international, there are audience interests that are worse or better served, and individuals who find that they do or do not want to use television. Television pleases some of the people all of the time, but not all of the people some of the time. Some nations, like Britain, are historically heavy in their per capita television usage when compared to others like France. However, the factors that make every nation's television specific are very difficult to grasp because they are so extensive. They are not to do with individual quirks, like a taste for on-screen continuity announcers or for variety shows, so much as with the architecture of the entire output. As such, they are not easily amenable to the traditional forms of content analysis, which privilege the systems of particular texts.

Each television system and each broadcaster within each system maintains a particular, shifting, balance between the genres of television. The key to the management of this process is the little understood activity of scheduling. The main networks in the USA have a relatively narrow generic mix, concentrated on news, talk, situation comedy and prime-time drama, and the same genres tend to be seen at the same time in the evening on each channel. Public service television tends to be defined by a wider range of genres so that head-to-head competition between programmes in the same genre is less habitual. Genres are the basic building blocks of television, and the schedule is the architecture that combines them. Everywhere the specific nature of television is defined by the schedule. The placing of particular programme types in relation to each other and to the predominant patterns of viewing habits; the balance between particular forms of programming; the choice of particular tendencies within those forms: these are the defining characteristics of every broadcast television service. The schedule defines the everyday specificity of television. Scheduling is nothing other than editing on an Olympian scale. Instead of combining shots and sounds into a sequence and sequences into a programme, as an editor does, the scheduler combines whole programme units into an evening's flow, whole evenings into a week, whole weeks into a season, and whole seasons into a year. The principles involved are broadly similar, combining variety and connection, repetition and originality into harmonious and mutually supporting arrangements. Just as editing involves a formidable activity of selection fundamental to the construction of any programme, scheduling defines the basic choices which define a broadcast television service.

The role of scheduling changed as the era of availability introduced greater complexity into the broadcasting system. The television industry in Britain was still referring to scheduling as 'the black art' as recently as 1985;[2] and only a decade later did the BBC begin to explain to its programme-makers the important process whereby schedulers specify programmes. For scheduling has been at the heart of a major change in the era of availability. Television has moved from an offer-led system to a demand-led system. In the era of scarcity, programme-makers generated ideas for programmes and offered them to their senior management. Management selected what they considered the best of these ideas, with an eye to the generic mix and the overall social purpose of their channel. The offers of ideas from programme-makers drove the whole system along. In the era of availability, this system has begun to atrophy. Instead, a demand-led system has developed. Now, the senior management of television specify the kinds of programming they need to fill particular slots in their schedule. The specification is in terms of budget, genre, target audience, and likely public image. The key mechanism in this process is the schedule. The demands generated by the process of scheduling now drive the broadcast television system.

In the era of scarcity, as we have seen in Chapter 4, scheduling consisted of little more than placing programmes in an order that reflected a broad division of the hours of the day into areas of presumed activity amongst the audience. The early evening, full of distractions and comings and goings, was the domain of news and magazine shows. As things settled down in the mid-evening, longer form programmes with more sustained storytelling were introduced; and the post-10.00pm period 'fringe zones' became an area of more experimentation leading into the low numbers and fragmentation of the late-night viewership. Broadcasting had set out on the road of providing a service in sympathy with the rhythms and practices of the daily lives of its audiences. As competition increased, so did the desire to know more about these rhythms and to cater for them better, or in a way that was distinct from competing channels. The pressure of everydayness, one of the defining features of broadcasting, gave a particular character to the competition between broadcast services. It was expressed through the growing importance of the scheduling process and fed through the use of increasingly sophisticated audience survey information.

Little has been written about the process of scheduling, but far more has been said about the use of audience survey information. Todd Gitlin, in *Inside Prime Time* is more keen to emphasize the inward-looking circularity of the scheduling process and how it uses the statistics that supposedly represent audience habits and preferences:

> As it is, the 'science' and the 'art' of program development and scheduling do only a few things for certain. They reinforce the networks' claim to be efficient servants of the popular will. Most important, they buttress network television's position as the most efficient medium for advertisers.[3]

This is a variant of the old truism that television exists to deliver audiences to advertisers. Elsewhere, however, Gitlin realizes that scheduling has a key role in the power structure of television:

> Since development executives move up by getting shows they've developed into the schedules, they make all the arguments about demography, time-slots, network suitability, lead-in, competition and advertiser zeal they can muster.[4]

Gitlin realizes that television understands and manages itself through the use and interpretation of statistical information about the audience. The most influential work in this area is Ien Ang's, which is centrally concerned with the broadcasters' obsession with demographics. Yet the word 'schedule' does not appear in the index of her *Desperately Seeking the Audience*.[5] There is also significant work on the division of time and the assumptions of viewing habits amongst the audience, but, again, this is not applied directly to an understanding of the process of scheduling.[6] There are good reasons, both polemical and academic, why this is the case. Critics have been concerned to argue for the relatively active nature of the audience, against the powerful commonplace that television is breeding nations of 'couch potatoes' and the more serious accusations that it conveys an uncritical 'dominant ideology'. At the same time, Ien Ang is careful to argue that statistical information about the audience fails to convey the cultural richness of the actual activity of viewing, especially its important emotional aspects. For, ultimately, television's audiences are unknowable.

So it is perfectly legitimate and important to criticize the television industry for its reliance on statistical audience data. But this will not change the industry's dependence on this data, because it provides the only available answer to the broadcasters' and advertisers' need to assess and predict the relationship between their programming and the everyday lives of their potential audiences.[7] So even as the industry admits the fictionality or untrustworthiness of the statistics, it continues to rely upon them. The figures have become a currency that circulates between competing broadcasting enterprises and their clients, be they advertisers seeking target markets or regulators seeking proof that public service broadcasting does indeed serve its public. However, the viewing figures do not only provide proof of past performance. For the broadcasters, they have a predictive power. On the basis of interpretations of these figures, the scheduling process determines the nature and type of programming to be offered to potential audiences. The schedule is the locus of power in television, the mechanism whereby demographic speculations are turned into a viewing experience. And it is more than that as well, for any schedule contains the distillation of the past history of a channel, of national broadcasting as a whole, and of the particular habits of national life.

The Nature of the Schedule

At its simplest, a schedule is a grid, dividing the broadcasting day into slots of thirty minutes' duration. Each slot is attributed a programme, ignoring the surrounding material of adverts, trailers, continuity announcements and the rest which are fitted in merely by making each programme shorter than its slot length. Even the definitive nature of this grid is a comparatively recent innovation. In the age of scarcity when much television was broadcast live, programme durations were difficult to control. In addition, the offer-led system and the definitive nature of individual programmes also validated the programme-makers' sense of the 'natural length' that a programme needed to have, so even filmed material tended to have idiosyncratic running times. But in the era of availability, individual programmes matter less than the integrity and the identity of the channel itself. So the schedule becomes a grid, consisting of regular time-slots to which programmes must conform.

The grid contains fixed points, programmes or genres that don't move. These are important moments in each channel's schedule and they reflect a number of important features: the inscribed assumptions about patterns of everyday lives; the tradition of the channel itself,[8] especially in the placing of the main news bulletins; and assumptions about the schedules of other channels. The actual grid pattern for any one channel has a number of virtual grids bearing down on it: the other grids relating to the week, the month, the season, the year; the grid of every other channel that is perceived as a competitor. In addition, schedulers need to bear in mind the pattern of competing domestic and non-domestic pursuits which vary from weekday to weekend and from season to season. This introduces a considerable level of complexity. Like all architecture, these are huge constructions, better lived in than expressed on paper. So how does scheduling work?

Planning a Schedule: From Statistics to Narratives

First, when a scheduler begins to plan a future season, there is always already a schedule that is to be changed, moulded and adapted. It consists of fixed features like news bulletins, which require a major policy debate to change, but otherwise simply of slots which have been filled in particular ways in the past, and need to be filled in the future. The performance of these current or recently past schedules can be assessed, and this is the principle guide to their possible future uses.

Each slot and programme is assessed using, principally, demographic data derived from the BARB (Broadcasters' Audience Research Bureau) audience surveys in the UK or the Neilsen ratings in the USA. Ratings have long since ceased to be a simple matter of numbers of viewers. They are highly sophisticated, claiming to provide details of the performance of particular programmes in particular slots on the grid. Numbers still matter in that they provide the bench-mark for the performance of the channel as a whole.[9] But overall audience numbers can only be increased by a subtle strategy of targeting particular sections of the audience for competing channels and providing something that will appeal to or satisfy them more (appeal and satisfaction being, in television at least, two different things). With the size of sample and techniques now used for audience measurement, audiences can be specified according to age, class, gender, region, pattern of viewing and even by their degree of appreciation of the programme.

In Britain, BARB works jointly for the broadcasters and the advertising industry. It costs 'well over ten million pounds a year to run'.[10] It is based on a panel of nearly 4500 homes, selected from an annual 'large-scale random probability survey of 40,000 homes – the annual Establishment Survey – which is conducted to supplement population details available from the Census. Using a device similar to a remote control, each person aged 4-plus in each panel home registers when he or she is in the room with the set switched on, so the record includes information on the viewing of roughly 11,500 individuals as well as on the use of sets.'[11] Provision is made for both time-shift videos and viewing by visitors. This information is retrieved silently by phone-link at the dead of night and initially processed in time to provide the crude 'overnights' to senior management at 10.00am the next day. Even this large demographic effort is beginning to break down: cable channels like the Parliament Channel do not register, and there is doubt about the entire sampling methodology for satellite/cable homes. But the system still works, better than the American Neilsen which for many years was slowed by its use of an automatic keypad system. However, the writing is on the wall for BARB as well. BARB's contract runs to 2002; by that date, fundamental reform will have to be devised if even this system, regarded as statistically robust, is to retain its relevance. This will be particularly difficult since there will not only be a proliferation of television channels by that date, but possibly also a proliferation of uses for the television as a domestic information terminal. The system has to deal with an unpredictable future, but also maintain the key importance of the current system. BARB's figures are open, shared by both advertisers and broadcasters.[12] BARB figures may be flawed even now, as BARB itself realizes. But it is acknowledged throughout the industry as having a basic validity, providing a reasonable picture of audience composition on a 15 minute by 15 minute basis. Even its sceptics use the statistics, which give them a formidable legitimacy.

With such a level of detailed 'knowledge' about the audience, the old adage 'television delivers audiences to advertisers', which was always simplistic, has to be re-written. At its very least, scheduling delivers programmes to audiences when they are most likely to want to watch them; and delivers audiences to advertisers in the composition that makes their advertising most likely to be effective. Across the day, the evening, the week and the month, the level of detail provided by BARB is extraordinary and even perhaps counterproductive. For the schedulers have to undertake a considerable degree of interpretation in order to deal with the figures. From the plethora of detail, they first construct a narrative of the audience for themselves. Using the overnights, they tell a story replete with the jargon of the trade, rather as a football fan will recount the story of a match. Channel controllers and schedulers see 'pre-echoes' and 'echoes' (audiences brought in before and staying after top rating shows) which they hope will provide an inheritance, and perhaps even maintain an audience across the 'junction points', the main evening breaks (for example, 9.00pm) where all channels end programmes and shift in gear. These junction points provide the opportunity to find new recruits as well. They have 'tent pole' programmes, the 'bankers' which provide a dependable lift to the graph of audience share. The schedulers identify the predominant demographics of the mass audience rating successes of their competitors and aim to make 'strategic hits' by providing programming that will appeal to and thus 'peel away' particular audience groupings. Where a synergy between channels exists (as with BBC1 and BBC2) they can indulge in 'complementary scheduling', a courtesy that was once also extended to protect elements of public service programming on competing channels, and to take advantage of audiences 'at a loose end'. For instance, the BBC now looks back with regret at the loss of its 'nursery' for new sitcoms: on Mondays at 8.30pm, when ITV used to show its current affairs flagship *World in Action*. But now that competition is more fierce, such practices have been abandoned, and the channels, like rampant stags, 'go head to head'. In such an atmosphere, like Britain in the mid-1990s, the received wisdom is that 'there are no safe areas in the schedule any more'.

So a narrative is constructed about the ebbs and flows of audiences for each evening's viewing. The figures are scanned for the successes and failures. For instance, a new show on Channel 4 at 8.00pm might have successfully reduced the pre-echo effect of BBC2's *Food and Drink*, and made a useful demographic hit amongst the key ELVs (Elusive Light Viewers). They might, through the careful placing of trailers, then be tempted to switch their TV back on to watch a historical documentary at 9.00pm. Strategies are assessed, continued or abandoned. In January 1998, Peter Salmon at BBC1 decided to start a strong documentary serial *The Cruise* on Tuesday at 8.00pm (20 January) followed by the second episode on Wednesday at 8.00pm. The calculation was simple: the series had a strong core of storytelling and compelling characters, which would

tempt viewers back. Salmon had detected a possible weak point in
ITV's Wednesday night schedule. After the 'banker' soap *Coronation
Street* at 7.30 they were showing *Des O'Connor Tonight*, described in
the listings as 'the popular entertainment show ... featuring celebrity
interviews, music, comedy and surprises'.[13] Salmon and his team
suspected that there was an audience for stories, for soap-like series,
which could be tempted across from ITV to watch *The Cruise*. They
interpreted the overnight figures on the morning of Thursday 22
January as proving that such an audience movement did take place,
so *The Cruise* stayed in the schedule on Tuesdays and Wednesdays at
8.00pm.[14]

Once such stories have been read from the figures, they are fed
into the activity of future scheduling. The level of demographic
detail provided by BARB enables schedulers to define slots according to the expected composition of their audience. Further, they can
specify the kinds of audiences that they would desire. In this, of
course, they receive a crucial input from the advertising industry,
which also has desirable demographics.

The Beeb Takes on The Bill 1: Friday Night

The practice of scheduling is more than simply the activity of placing
programmes to best effect. An examination of a particular question
within the BBC will show how powerful scheduling is in the management of television, and how much it defines the nature of
broadcast output in the era of availability. For many years, the BBC's
mass audience channel BBC1 had a problem in maintaining or
increasing its audience share against the strong programmes in the
early evening ITV schedule. These are the long-running soap
Coronation Street[15] and the police series *The Bill*, which centres on Sun
Hill police station in London. During the period 1995-97, the format
of *The Bill* was one of dealing with a single crime in each half-hour
episode, and tracing the development of Sun Hill station and its core
characters for months at a time. During 1995, BBC1 tried two
different strategies to combat the drawing power of *The Bill* in ITV's
schedules, one on Thursday nights, and the other on Fridays. Each
strategy depended upon different analyses of the source of the

attraction of *The Bill* to its audiences. But a healthy dose of accident played its part as well.

Both *The Bill* and *Coronation Street* have strong audience loyalties; they are the 'bankers' of the ITV early evening. There was little that the BBC felt it could do against *Coronation Street*, but they thought that *The Bill* presented a possible target. On Friday evenings, uniquely, they were scheduled together. For several years, ITV's Friday evening had shown *Coronation Street* at 7.30, followed by *The Bill* at 8.00: a 'killer combination'. The echo and pre-effect of *The Bill*, preceded by the Friday episode of *Coronation Street*, meant that BBC1's entire Friday evening audience was reduced, and for years the ITV 'won' Friday evening. For some years, the best strategy that BBC1 controllers could offer was to repeat much-loved sitcoms like *Only Fools and Horses* or *Porridge* in the 8.00pm slot.

In 1995, a fresh strategy was tried to 'peel off' audience sectors from this massive audience, targeting *The Bill* not because it was necessarily more 'vulnerable' but simply because it came second and so could create an inheritance for the following 8.30 show. Against *Coronation Street* BBC1 has, variously, gone 'head to head' with an edition of its soap *Eastenders*, and 'gone niche' by putting *Top of the Pops* at 7.30. Neither strategy has been a conspicuous success. On Easter Friday, 14 April 1995, Alan Yentob, then controller of BBC1, tested out the 'factual entertainment' series *999 Lifesavers*, which reconstructs medical emergencies, in the BBC1 8.00pm Friday slot. It had been performing well in an 8.00pm Monday slot against ITV's *The Bill*. Although both programmes were based around the emergency services, *The Bill*'s audience demographic profile, Yentob had been told, showed it to be weighted towards a middle-aged audience. *999 Lifesavers* and other such factually based entertainments performed better, perhaps surprisingly, than did the sitcoms which BBC1 had initially pitched against *The Bill*. Info-tainment has a younger demographic profile. The results of this cautious Good Friday test looked auspicious. So on 15 September 1995 the effective *Bill*-competitor *999 Lifesavers* moved to compete against it on Friday evening, which it did for a total of nine weeks until 17 November. However, the programme did noticeably less well on Fridays against *The Bill* than it had done on Mondays. *999 Lifesavers* did not reappear in the 8.00pm slot after the *Children in Need* telethon of 24 November 1995, and was played in the spring 1996 season at 9.30 on Fridays. At the time, the exercise seemed to prove the power of the schedule sequence to build and maintain audiences. Within BBC scheduling culture, the example of the Friday stand-off between *The Bill* and *999 Lifesavers* has entered the professional discourse as an example of the power of ITV's scheduling and of 'inheritance' in particular.[16]

But, with hindsight, there are probably other reasons for the failure of this particular strategy. They include the nature of the Friday night audience; the variations in quality and audience appeal of the *999 Lifesavers* series concerned; and even the degree of promotion given to the programmes. Above all, it was likely that the similarities of subject matter between the two series were too pronounced. The in-trade generic definition of 'flashing blue light programming' was becoming widely used by television listings publications around this time. This demonstrates one of the problems with a scheduling process driven by the narrativizing of audience statistics. When a programme in a particular genre has proved a success, more material in the same genre will be commissioned – by all the competing channels – in an attempt to reduplicate the success at 'peeling off' the same audience segment elsewhere. In the end, this leads to a generic imbalance, perceived by critics and public as a 'sudden glut' of a particular kind of programming. Indeed, there may well be proof that this was the case. The same strategy was tried again two years later by Michael Jackson, during his brief tenure as Controller of BBC1. From 17 October to 19 December 1997, *999 Lifesavers* ran against *The Bill* with more success: it returned in the same slot after the interruption of the *Children in Need* telethon of 21 November 1997. By that time, 'flashing blue lights' had become a less predominant feature of television's output as a whole.

The Beeb Takes on The Bill 2: Thursday Night

Another attempt by the BBC to combat the power of *The Bill*, this time on Thursday evenings, was more successful, and indeed opened the way to an innovation in cross-generic programming. In the previous case, BBC1's schedulers had assumed that *The Bill's* continuing success hinged upon its nature as a police drama. But on another evening, a different analysis of the power of *The Bill* was being tested:

> We analysed the demographics of *The Bill* and discovered that it was much closer to a soap than we had imagined. ... Our stroke of luck was *Animal Hospital*. For almost serendipitous reasons, it was played against *The Bill* where it was extremely successful.' *Animal Hospital* was commissioned to fill the 8pm slot, and did 'considerable damage' to ITV.[17]

Initially, *Animal Hospital Week* had been a weekly 'stripped' special event, which followed the work of a vet's practice, fronted by Rolf Harris, by then an over-the-hill children's presenter. Showing in the last week of August 1994, it had played at 6.10pm on the Bank Holiday Monday, and thereafter at 8.00pm Tuesday to Friday. It was the quintessence of popular public service broadcasting as the BBC conceives it, providing information about animal care within an entertaining format. After its unexpected success, it was recommissioned as a weekly half hour for Thursdays at 8.00pm from 12 January 1995, again against *The Bill*. In this new weekly form, it had more pronounced soap aspects. It developed regular characters, plenty of chat and speculation and week to week cliff-hanger suspense about 'how the animals will do'. Against *The Bill*, its demographic was markedly younger and more female, because of its 'furry animal' subject. Its dramatic form was fairly close to the soap aspects of *The Bill*, and, if anything, intensified them. It provided a greater use of the cliff-hanger between episodes, something which *The Bill* lacked with its structure of a separate single case each episode. As the *Radio Times* of 4-10 March 1995 announced, *Animal Hospital* was successful enough in this slot to be extended.

The case of *Animal Hospital* is important not only because of its success but because of its consequences. Wildlife documentaries, like *Wildlife on One* or *Nature Detectives*, had long been a mainstay of the BBC1 Thursday schedule at 8.00pm. But *Animal Hospital* was something new. It was as much a soap as a factual programme, and it seemed to appeal to that part of the audience which responded to the soap aspects of *The Bill* without having a wholehearted enthusiasm for the 'flashing blue light' subject. The chance performance of *Animal Hospital* against *The Bill* created the specification of a programme to run against it in the forthcoming season: a factual, soap-structured, feminine-subject series. As Docherty says, 'this, coupled with a stream of successful factual programmes, has been our great success.'[18] In other words, we can date from this moment the beginnings of the generic development of documentary soaps, or 'docutainment' with strong soap narrative habits.

This shows how important scheduling has become as the location of the key management decisions in broadcast television. A scheduling process that interpreted demographic data produced the demand for a docu-tainment series. Further demographic data about its subsequent performance was interpreted as proving correct the scheduler's analysis, which deduced that *The Bill* was providing only partial satisfaction to a significant part of its audience. This in turn provoked the ordering of further 'fly on the wall' documentary series with strong soap aspects as a new element in peak time scheduling in the late 1990s. *Animal Hospital* was followed a string of similar series like *Vets in Practice, Animals in Uniform, Pet Rescue*. Then in summer of 1997 came *Driving School* , which gathered an audience of up to 12 million, and created a minor celebrity in headstrong and incompetent Maureen Rees, who had multiple test failures to her credit. *Driving School*'s success confirmed the suspicion of schedulers and programme-makers that documentary and soap could be combined simply by following individuals in particular circumstances, so long as they were exhibitionist enough. So there followed *Hotel, Cruise, Clampers* (about traffic wardens) and then BBC1's *Paddington Green*, whose eccentrics were linked simply by the fact that they lived in the same district. Perhaps, had *999 Lifesavers* performed as well as *Animal Hospital* against *The Bill*, peak time would now be filled by reconstructions of gruesome events: but it was not to be. Instead, the new (and inexpensive) sub-genre of docu-soap was so successful that by the beginning of 1998, the first signs of an industry backlash were beginning to appear, pointing to the possibility of a new generic imbalance.[19] It will probably be another temporary fashion, like the glut of chat shows in the 1980s (*Wogan, Jonathan Ross, Clive Anderson Talks Back*).

Schedules Order Programmes

Scheduling creates the demand for programmes. The schedule will identify a target audience size for each slot, and consequently will specify a particular demographic profile. The target is not simply a matter of numbers but also of their expected composition. This then provides the mechanism through which a number of consequent key decisions are made. The schedule provides for the balance between genres. It finds the 'best slot' for already known programmes, or ones that have been more successful (demographically as well as in overall figures) than their slot would seem to justify. These are the elusive successes that have 'outperformed their slot'. Then, overall numbers and the demographic will determine what the slot is worth in terms of programme budget. So the schedule is the planning mechanism that determines the balance between genres and levels of cost across the channel as a whole. The schedule therefore drives the planning of output. It used to put programmes in order. Now, in the American phrase, it 'orders programmes' from the producers.

Nowadays, this planning process uses data gathered from beyond the basic BARB statistics. ITV and the BBC have begun to test pilots for new programmes, or even – in the case of ITV – the concepts for new programmes, with focus groups.[20] This is a practice new to British television in the late 1990s, reflecting a greater degree of perceived competition within the system. Pilots are routinely made for new formats, which are shown to focus groups first to assess their reaction as a sample audience (much like a Hollywood preview of a feature film) and then to gauge their overall opinions through discussions of a more or less directed nature. These help the further development of the format. Drama series present a more difficult case, as it is almost impossible to produce a pilot to assess their mise-en-scene, and, as they depend upon their mise-en-scene so crucially, concept-based research would yield little of interest. However, dramas are often shown to focus groups after their completion. Such viewings serve two purposes: they guide the marketing strategy for the series, and, inevitably perhaps, yield 'tips for a second series'.[21] Focus groups are constructed to reflect the target demographic. They are probed not only about the desirability for them of the pilots they are shown, but also about their own domestic viewing habits. Questions might include: 'Would you watch this at 7.00 or at 8.00 or at 9.00?'; 'What programme is this closest to for you?'; 'Would you watch it in preference to...?'; and might even extend to the perceived appeal of the show, 'Would your granny like it?' or 'Would your mum be appalled?' The attempt here is to delve behind demographics into the practical habits of living and the 'personal schedules' that everyone carries with them (the 'familiarity factor').[22]

For although there is much quantitative information involved in the process of scheduling, it is still riddled with uncertainty. Any one schedule is the result of choices conceived in an atmosphere of

competition and uncertainty. Any one schedule is being 'attacked'
from a number of sides. First, there are the direct competitor
channels. In Britain these are the terrestrial broadcast channels:
BBC1 and ITV, BBC2, Channel 4 and Channel 5. Even the mass
channels of BBC1 and ITV face a significant level of competition
from the minority channels which seek to 'peel off' particular
demographics, for example the practice of BBC2 and Channel 4 of
showing youth-oriented shows (like *Star Trek* reruns on BBC2 or the
teenage soap opera *Hollyoaks* on Channel 4) when BBC1 and ITV
are showing their early evening news around 6.00pm. In addition,
the practice of other television channels, the satellite BSkyB channels
and those available on cable or through new digital delivery formats,
has to be taken into account as they are making inroads into the
audience for terrestrial broadcast television. Indeed, schedulers are
aware that television is a very crowded market, and that the competition for the total TV viewing time of individuals sometimes leads
to the perception that there are 'just too many things on tonight'.
Beyond all of this lies the unpredictable universe of the household's
living and viewing patterns, with its personality clashes and power
struggles which are often expressed around the use of television.
Finally, of course, there are further other demands on leisure time in
general.[23]

Scheduling attempts to 'deal with' all the aspects of competition,
while not knowing what most will be. So it is a rolling planning
process, in which all plans are adjusted as more intelligence comes
in, particularly about the probable strategies of the opposition.[24]
Scheduling is about managing the ever-present nature of television.
It uses the immediate past as its most powerful referent in attempting to define the immediate future, and so to order the output for
that future. However, there is a basic problem with the whole
process: as Ien Ang points out, it is self-enclosed. The analytic tools
being used – the BARB survey – are self-validating. The success or
failure of a particular scheduling strategy is measured by the same
methodology that suggested it in the first place. A problem with the
audience size or composition produced by a particular programming
policy is identified through using the BARB figures. This leads to
changes in that policy, whose success is measured by using the same
BARB data. So any systematic discrepancy between the system of
measurement (the statistics produced by BARB) and what is measured (the behaviour of real audiences) will remain undetected.

There seem to be just two external moderators on this inward-looking system. Both of them are essentially unsystematic. The first is the amount and character of the coverage given to a programme (or a performer) by the press. This coverage can be interpreted in a number of ways. Favourable coverage in particular publications (mainly those with an ELV or youth demographic slant) can be interpreted as indicating that the series is a 'sleeper': one that will increase in popularity as it goes on. *Absolutely Fabulous*, initially aired on BBC2, was a classic example of this tendency in Britain, as was *Hill Street Blues* in the USA.[25] Coverage in the broadsheet press or in upmarket weekly magazines can be seen as a mark of prestige, which might well accord with the corporate aims of a public service broadcaster or the commercial aims of a channel aiming to generate advertising revenue through addressing an upmarket demographic.

The press is a relatively public form of moderation of the statistics-led approach to scheduling. The other is more capricious, consisting of anecdotal evidence gathered by senior broadcasters themselves. Parodied as 'My driver told me...', it is much more likely to take the form of 'My nanny says her friends think that...'. In a highly compartmentalized society, such a random factor can gain a disproportionate influence, and, indeed, the more general questions addressed to focus groups are intended to open up such information more systematically. But such insights are used randomly. On an everyday basis, scheduling seeks to prove how it is working by reference almost exclusively to the work of BARB, by building narratives of audience behaviour out of the demographic data.

Scheduling is the point where the activity of the past and the hopes of the present become the strategy for the future. It is the point where television's everydayness encounters its competitive nature. The sum total of schedules, locked in their competitive struggle, defines the character of a national television economy, or, to be more accurate, the character of a particular broadcasting market. From this perspective, the character of the national scheduling battle constitutes a formidable site of resistance and resilience in face of any globalizing tendencies that might bear down upon it. For television is always specific, however much it may be amenable to generalizations. In every television system, national or international, there are audience interests that are worse or better served; individuals who find that they do or do not want to use television; genres that are over-used and genres that are neglected. The activity of competitive scheduling will ensure that this is the case.

---

[1] See Andrea Millwood Hargrave (ed), *The Scheduling Game* (London: John Libbey and Company Ltd, 1995), pp 9-73.

[2] See, for example, the press coverage of Michael Grade's arrival at Channel 4.

[3] Todd Gitlin, *Inside Prime Time* (London: Routledge, 1994), p 62.

[4] *Ibid.*, p 59.

[5] Ang's concern is not with the way that the institutions of television operate so much as with the ways that audiences use what television offers. Hence her more recent statement: 'We must come to the conclusion that any attempt to construct positive knowledges about the "real consumer" will always be provisional, partial, fictional. This is not to postulate the total freedom of television viewers. Far from it. It is, however, to foreground and dramatise the continuing dialectic between the technologised strategies of the industry and the fleeting and dispersed tactics by which consumers, while confined by the offerings provided by the industry, sureptitiously seize moments to transform these offerings into "opportunities" of their own.' *Living Room Wars* (London: Routledge, 1996), p 64. My argument here is not with this perspective. I am examining the area covered by the phrase 'while confined by the offerings provided by the industry'.

[6] See for example Roger Silverstone, *Television and Everyday Life* (London: Routledge, 1994); Paddy Scannell, *Radio, Television and Modern Life: A Phenomenological Approach* (Oxford: Basil Blackwell, 1996), especially chapter 7, and John Caughie's interesting remarks in his essay in Patricia Mellencamp (ed), *Logics of Television: Essays in Cultural Criticism* (Bloomington: University of Indiana and London: British Film Institute, 1990), p 49, which provide an important insight into what is already a historical era in British scheduling, comparing it with the USA.

[7] For further views on audience data, see Bob Mullan, *Consuming Television* (Oxford: Basil Blackwell, 1997); David Morley, *Family Television: Cultural Power and Domestic Leisure* (London: Routledge, 1988); 'On the audience' in Silverstone: *Television and Everyday Life*; or Shaun Moores, *Interpreting Audiences: The Ethnography of Media Consumption* (London: Sage Publications, 1993).

[8] 'The schedule is as it is because we've had "The Street" for 37 years and "News" [At Ten] for going on 30. That's served us well, so if we're to make changes we won't do it in 100 days.' David Liddiment, ITV Network Director of Programmes, interviewed by Mundy Ellis, *Televisual*, February 1998, p 18. In fact, it took Liddiment almost a year to move the main ITV news bulletin from the *News at Ten* slot to a later slot (and shorter duration) at 11.00pm.

[9] For example, early in 1998 ITV set itself target figures for its audience share for the future in response to a decline in its overall audience figures.

[10] All quotations in this account taken from a highly informative article by the ITC's Director of Research Bob Towler, *Spectrum* (the now defunct quarterly of the ITC), Spring 1996, pp 12-13.

[11] *Ibid.*

[12] However, the broadcasters have commissioned their own bolt-on extra, for their eyes only: the Appreciation Ratings. On a scale of 1-10, the panel, through a diary system, rate their enjoyment of programmes. The majority of programmes get an 8; I once produced a programme that scored 5: *The Holy Family Album* written by Angela Carter for Channel 4, December 1991.

[13] *Radio Times*, 21 January 1998.

[14] Peter Salmon addressing the Independent Commissioning Department's Open Day, BBC TV Centre, 9 February 1998.

[15] On *Coronation Street*, see, for example, Richard Dyer (ed), *Coronation Street* (London: BFI Publishing, 1981), and Christine Geraghty, *Women and Soap Opera: A Study of Prime Time Soaps* (Cambridge: Polity Press, 1991).

[16] My source is a speech to independent producers by Alan Yentob in January 1996.

[17] David Docherty, then Head of BBC TV Planning and Strategy, 'Confessions of a justified scheduler' in Millwood Hargrave: *The Scheduling Game*, p 126.

[18] *Ibid.*, p 125.

[19] 'With all this fly on the wall stuff, we are in danger of being swamped ... there is a new popular factual programme every week. Soon we are going to have some disasters. I hope they are BBC disasters and not ITV disasters.' Ian Lewis (Zenith Media, buyers), *Broadcast*, 16 January 1998, p 5.

[20] The use of focus group testing began in British television at the same time as it became common in British politics. For an analysis of the increased use of focus groups in the political arena, see P. Gould, *The Unfinished Revolution: How the Modernisers Saved the Labour Party* (London: Little, Brown, 1998).

[21] Tessa Ross, comments on the BBC1 series *Playing the Field*, written by Kay Mellor, BBC Independents commissioning meeting, 9 January 1998.

[22] See Millwood Hargrave: *The Scheduling Game*, pp 9-26.

[23] For example, on Saturday 7 June 1997, the audience for the National Lottery draw on BBC1 'collapsed' from a normal 11-13 million to a little over 6 million. The demise of the Lottery as a national obsession was widely predicted. However, the reason was entirely different: it was the first good day of weekend weather for almost a month, after an unusually cold and wet May; an England v. France football match was being broadcast at the same time as the draw; and the afternoon's sport had included the Derby and a Test Match. Sure enough, the next week's *Lottery Live* audience was back above 11 million.

[24] See, for example, Docherty: 'Confessions' for a tale of last minute scheduling changes.

[25] For a comprehensive analysis of the commissioning of *Hill Street Blues*, see chapter 14 of Gitlin: *Inside Prime Time*.

CHAPTER 10

CHANNEL 4: FROM OFFER-LED TO DEMAND-LED TELEVISION

Since it began broadcasting in 1982, Britain's Channel 4 has been celebrated around the world as an outstanding example of a successful experimental television service. But it was very much a product of the complicated times in which it was set up, and has had great difficulties in adjusting to the new realities of television in the age of availability. This is ironic since it was Channel 4 itself that did more than any other television organization to move British television into the new era. Channel 4 was crucial in breaking open the habits of the era of scarcity, in leading the development away from concepts of balance and towards that of diversity of view. Yet at the same time, Channel 4's commissioning structure was the most extreme example of the offer-led system of television production. With no significant programme-making capacity of its own, Channel 4 relied – and still relies – entirely on the programme ideas that it is offered by independent producers. As a result, it has found particular difficulties in adapting to the developments in scheduling practice described in the last chapter.[1]

The Roots of Channel 4

During the 1960s, two notions of quality television began to emerge. An earlier idea, that quality was associated with cultural values borrowed from the arts, remained strong. Many people continued to believe that quality television was the broadcasting of classical music concerts, opera, adaptations of stage drama and educational documentaries. PBS, the Public Broadcasting System in America added its own twist to this, aided by some tendencies in the BBC. For them, quality was associated with budget: a quality documentary series like Kenneth Clark's *Civilisation* in 1969 combined high ideals with high budgets. Quality drama became confused with high-cost drama, with the writer-led experiments of live TV drama of the 1950s like ITV's *Armchair Theatre* or the BBC's *Wednesday Play* giving way increasingly to expensive, film-like drama and showy costume drama like ITV's *Brideshead Revisited* of 1981. This was one, increasingly conservative, definition of quality.

Another began to emerge towards the end of the era of scarcity in Britain during the 1970s which stressed the social values incarnated in programmes more than their cost or even (at times) their technical proficiency. This definition of quality stressed both citizenship and creativity. It saw quality as providing a varied service which enhanced the life of the citizens and enabled them to participate more fully in their society. It also stressed the importance of innovation in keeping in touch with the audience, in order to avoid making predictable programmes and to continue to engage and surprise their audiences. This definition of quality became more and more predominant among programme-makers in the 1970s as a reaction to the social changes which swept through the First World in the 1960s. It was not an entirely revolutionary idea, however. Programme-makers were still a privileged social group seeking to legislate for the tastes of their fellow citizens. But, unlike their predecessors, they felt themselves to be excluded from the centres of power. Their self-image was one of being 'anti-establishment', of holding liberal or radical ideas and of being openly critical of many older cultural values. 'Innovation' became the rallying cry of such people, within and beyond television, and it produced a powerful critique of much of the programming being shown on British television, often couched in terms of how different kinds of people were represented on television. The critique saw racism and sexism as being rife in entertainment and present even in the more liberal of documentaries. And, looking back, it was justified.

In the 1960s, the first stirrings of this critique were used creatively by the inauguration of BBC2 in 1964, a second BBC channel whose brief was to make programmes for minority tastes which were being badly catered for by BBC1 and ITV. These channels commanded large audiences, often up to 40 per cent of the British public. This was still the era of television scarcity, after all, when choice was a matter of either BBC or ITV or nothing at all. So BBC2 produced such innovatory documentary programmes as *Man Alive*, which trod a careful line between respect and salaciousness in its coverage of social problems. The uniqueness of *Man Alive* in 1965 was the role it gave to the ordinary men and women of Britain. They were accorded a new respect and dignity. Instead of being brought on as evidence for the propositions of legislators and academics, they were allowed to speak their feelings and beliefs directly, within a structure provided by discreet editing and commentary. As Chapter 8 has discussed, these early programmes sometimes found it difficult to judge the point at which revelation gave way to exploitation. However, the way that they demonstrated a new respect for ordinary citizens was the precursor in Britain of a fundamental shift in broadcasting away from the values and perspectives of cultural elites towards the broadcasting system of today. However, the shift was long in coming. By the mid-1970s, *Man Alive* was no more, and BBC2 interpreted its responsibility towards minority tastes in two ways. One was the provision of coverage of sport and hobbies which were not covered on the two main channels: golf, snooker and sheepdog trials; gardening, motoring and archaeology. Otherwise, the more conservative notion of quality television was in ascendance: costume drama, expensive documentaries and intellectual conversation. The critique of broadcasting behind the newer notion of quality seemed to have passed the BBC by. Not for the first time in its history, the organization was widely perceived as complacent and distant from the audiences that it was meant to serve.

This, then, was the context in which Channel 4 was invented. Two mass audience channels faced each other in nightly competition. The one minority channel had wedded itself to the tastes of the elite. A powerful critique of the fundamental values of broadcasting amongst its own programme-makers had produced a fresh conception of quality, based on the idea of 'innovation'. So the project for a fourth television channel was examined, as things were done then, by a Royal Commission chaired by Lord Annan. It took evidence from all who wished to offer it, aiming to produce a series of recommendations for a new television channel. In 1977, the Annan Commission concluded that the new channel should be independent of both ITV and the BBC, and that it should be a 'publisher broadcaster', showing programmes but not making them itself, an idea that is generally ascribed to Anthony Smith.[2] However, before this revolutionary idea could be implemented, another momentous event took place: the general election of 1979 which brought Margaret Thatcher to power.

The Construction of Channel 4

Margaret Thatcher's election victory in 1979 is remembered as a sea change in British politics. The 1970s had been characterized by often painful attempts to construct a wide political consensus for actions in a context where the major groups in society – workers and employers; middle classes; ethnic groups; English, Scots and Welsh; young and old; men and women – were drifting apart. Thatcher's form of conservatism replaced government by consensus with a far more doctrinaire and authoritarian form of government. This was a new experience for Britain, and 1979 is remembered as a point of harsh change, especially as the early Thatcher years were characterized by some spectacular economic mismanagement resulting in a crisis in 1981. However, the shift from consensus to authoritarianism was in practice more gradual. The case of Channel 4 demonstrates this, as the Annan Commission's vision of a publisher-broadcaster came into being through a spectacular piece of consensus politics.

In the Channel 4 project, many different readings of the same ideas coalesced together. In independent production, the emerging forces of the Thatcher government saw small businesses which could act as a crusading force against the restrictive labour and management practices of 1960s and 1970s television. Older consensus politicians saw a way of bringing socially marginalized voices into the arena of broadcasting. And programme-makers themselves saw, variously, the possibility of making programmes without heavy and everyday editorial interference and the chance to make a good deal of money. Even ITV, which had campaigned for an ITV2 to match

BBC2, came away relatively satisfied. The Channel 4 which emerged from all of this was a bold experiment. It was to be a commercial channel, reliant on advertising revenue, but devoted to 'tastes and interests not catered for by ITV' and to 'innovation and experiment in the form and the content of programmes', both of which were at the time seen as completely anti-commercial propositions. In addition, it was to take half of its original programming from independent production companies. Few such companies actually existed and none of them had any significant record of producing television programmes before, outside advertising or the film industry. This was not surprising since the existing British broadcasters made the whole of their output apart from the programmes that they bought from abroad (which meant, in practice, from the USA).

The art of political compromise exercised by William Whitelaw, the government minister responsible for the legislation, is clear in the unique mechanisms of support offered to this experimental channel. It was not, like many other doomed experiments, to be reliant on its own commercial income from the launch day. A funding mechanism was put in place which took into account many of ITV's complaints about its recent legislative treatment. The regional companies which made up ITV had made so much money from their operations that a special 'excess profits' tax had been introduced as a payment for their right to broadcast. Whitelaw proposed that a proportion of this tax should contribute to supporting Channel 4. In return, the ITV companies would have the right to sell advertising space on the new channel and keep the proceeds, free of excess profits tax. This proved an acceptable deal, especially when, after five years, some of the ITV companies began to make a profit on it. In addition, ITV was to provide half of the new channel's programming, and to be paid the going rate for doing so. This provided a dependable source of programming for Channel 4, and a useful means of using up spare capacity for the ITV companies. In all, it was a complex compromise, but one which provided Channel 4 with the crucial elements it needed to become a success. The first of these elements was time, since no target date was set for the Channel to become self-sufficient. The second was financial stability, since the funding arrangements with ITV provided a predictable income. Few other experimental channels have had such an auspicious start, and Whitelaw's formula is the key to Channel 4's long-term success.[3]

The appointment of Jeremy Isaacs as the first Chief Executive of Channel 4 was the other key. Isaacs was given a blueprint for a company within a regulatory regime set by the Independent Broad-casting Authority (which also regulated ITV), but nothing more than that. He developed the idea of commissioning editors: individuals entrusted with a budget and the responsibility for buying pro-grammes from independent companies on the basis of proposals sent in by them. This sealed the identity of Channel 4 as the most extreme example of the offer-led system of television management. Under Isaacs, commissioning editors had considerable freedom to define policy in their areas of programming.[4] Michael Kustow, responsible for arts, declared that he would commission no docu-mentaries about the arts, preferring instead to place performances before the audience including such extravagances as Peter Brook's *Mahabharata*. Alan Fountain, responsible for 'Independent Film and Video' (a euphemism for the avant-garde of all kinds) commissioned some of the boldest experiments in the channel's output as well as some of its most dire moments. But this was, in Isaacs' opinion, the essence of experiment: it required a degree of failure to produce its successes. Fountain's output therefore ranged from political films from the Third World to formalist avant-garde work from Britain and the USA. The freedom of the commissioning editor within an agreed budget was crucial to Isaacs' strategy. Later on, this freedom was considerably reduced under Isaacs' successor Michael Grade.

Isaacs' founding management team also realized that independent companies would be unable to finance productions from their own funds, and that, if they used bank loans, the interest payable would waste crucial production funds. So Channel 4's financial team developed a system whereby the companies were advanced funds when needed according to an agreed budget and cash-flow. The companies received a set percentage of the budget on successful completion of the programmes. This had the advantage of giving security to small independent companies as well as providing an intimate relationship between the channel and its commissions. This 'cost-plus' system was crucial in underpinning many experiments and bold new initiatives in programme-making, the vast majority of which were the product of Channel 4's offer-led system, picking and choosing from the ideas offered by independent companies.

Channel 4 began broadcasting in November 1982. A decade later, the Broadcasting Act of 1992 cut the ties between Channel 4 and ITV, and left Channel 4 to subsist on its advertising revenues alone. In financial terms, it has done so supremely well. By 1998, Channel 4 had become a feature of the British broadcasting environment, watched by a regular 10 to 12 per cent of the audience viewing terrestrial TV (itself 90 per cent of the total viewing audience), on the same level as BBC2. Many of the expectations of the varied proponents of the publisher-broadcaster model had been realized. British television programmes had changed, to a significant degree as a result of Channel 4. Gone were the condescending and stereotyped portrayals criticized in the 1970s. Programmes were more diverse, and almost the full extent of British society was present on British television. (As for the rest of the world, however, that remains a different matter.) The independent producers made a success of their brief: many made programmes of the kind that they had always dreamed of making (and others the money that they had dreamed of). And independent production has transformed the way in which the television industry works by gaining access to both BBC and ITV commissions.

Channel 4 was born from a coalition of ideas about quality. Establishment figures like William Whitelaw probably assumed that Channel 4 would finally provide him with programmes about fishing (which it did), and the increasingly vocal political and social minorities left out of traditional politics assumed that they would get their say on the new channel (and in the early days they did). But when Channel 4 started broadcasting, each interest group saw the other's programming as somehow betraying the original purpose of the channel. For Channel 4 was beginning to lead the adaptation of British television to the emerging age of television: the era of availability.

Away from the Habits of Scarcity

Channel 4's opening night revealed the mixture of expectations it was to satisfy. The opening programme, *Countdown*, was a simple panel game asking contestants to assemble words from arbitrarily chosen letters. The show still runs, and has a large following among retired people seeking intellectual stimulation: a significant and neglected minority in most broadcasting contexts. Later came the first edition of the soap opera *Brookside*, set in a Liverpool housing estate, and using real houses as its set and a vividness of language and plot that marked it out from other soap operas. A comedy spoof

Five Go Mad in Dorset showed a commitment to new comic talent, and the film *Walter* a commitment to the development of a British art cinema which would not avoid depressing topics. In between, there had been a twenty-five minute *Opinion* programme consisting of an individual with an argument to put speaking straight to camera, and an hour-long *Channel 4 News*. The commitments were all there, along with their faults as well as their virtues. In some programmes, particularly *Opinion*, the poverty of resources was all too evident, yet the attempt was both welcome and vital.

Channel 4 was the first channel on British television to abandon one of the central tenets of the era of broadcasting scarcity: the idea of balance. When few channels existed, and they broadcast only a few hours each day, then it followed that each programme should have something definitive about it. Whether documentary or drama, it should attempt a thorough articulation of a problem or a character, and avoid the partial, polemical or tendentious. Balance was the key concept that kept broadcasting free of political interference during the years of compromise government, and balance meant the avoidance of programmes which put distinctive points of view. The problem was that very often this meant that programmes lacked an emotional drive and a sense of commitment. So one of the key elements in the call for 'diversity' in British television, the call which gave birth to Channel 4, was the idea that balance should be abandoned as the governing concept of broadcasting. Channel 4, and in particular its founding chief executive Jeremy Isaacs, argued often and long in its early days for the idea that balance should be seen as provided across the whole of its output rather than as within any one programme.[5] This freed its programmes to be far more the expressions of particular points of view, usually social rather than individual. Series were commissioned to put the views of the ethnic minorities in Britain: *Black on Black* and *Asian Eye*. Constant attempts were made to make a magazine programme for women, but these always seemed to fail. Later, gay series like *Out on Tuesday* were launched, breaking one of the great taboos of the British media. The key problem for all of these programmes was one of address: were they made for the groups with whom they were identified, or were they made from those groups for a wider public? More often than not, they wavered between the two forms of address, their very explicitness of focus becoming a problem for them.

This problem arose because these programmes were made at the beginning of a new phase of broadcasting. In the era of availability,

British audiences are far more used to the idea that no programme
will provide a definitive view of a question, the idea behind the
principle of balance. No one programme can contain the different
views which exist in British society, and they are no longer expected
to do so, since no one programme can be expected to reach more
than a small section of the population. So programmes are relieved
of the requirement of balance, but broadcasters are increasingly
facing another set of requirements: to represent the shifting diversity
of British society. In 1998, the BBC launched an audience research
project entitled 'The Hundred Tribes' which is attempting to develop
a picture of this diversity. The choice of the idea of 'tribe', encapsulating a sense of non-exclusive but strong allegiance, along with the
number of tribes envisaged, is indicative of the new nature of British
society.

Balance has given way to diversity. Television is no longer the
arbiter of content, but a forum for content. Channel 4 pushed the
boundaries of what it was possible to see on British television, and
hastened this process. It gave a place to programmes about world
cinema at a time when non-American films were becoming a rarity in
British cinemas. It showed angry films about animal rights; elegiacal
programmes about euthanasia; sharp satires about the production of
news like *Drop the Dead Donkey*; left-wing political thrillers like *A Very
British Coup*; situation comedies in novel settings like a West Indian
barber's shop (*Desmond's*); the whole of Claude Lansmann's series on
the Holocaust (*Shoa*); and a late-night discussion series that continued until the participants agreed to go home (*After Dark*). The early
years of Channel 4 were full of experiments in how to make a
different kind of television. Some, like the youth and music show
Whatever You Want crossed television boundaries so often that it was
in the end replaced. At the same time, these innovative and experimental programmes were surrounded by entirely conventional
programmes which addressed interests or audiences that were not
served elsewhere: photography, oil painting, fishing, travel and so on.
There were even broadcasts of operas. This was the distinctive mix
that gave birth to Channel 4 and ensured that it had 'something for
everyone'.

At first, the channel was attacked from many sides. The press,
hostile to a new competitor in the advertising market, could not
decide whether it was objectionable because of its unaccustomed
swearing (as in the epithet 'Channel Swore') or tedious because of its
long stretches of talking heads (as in 'Channel Bore'). Jeremy Isaacs

tells of his meeting with William Whitelaw after one year of broad-casting at which Whitelaw very politely asked him to restrain some of the more outrageous programmes in his output. Isaacs, in turn, excused this by reference to the remit for experimentation. Both sides knew what the other was asking for and why.[6] But in the end, it was wider forces working in television which altered Channel 4, after the departure of Jeremy Isaacs in 1987.

The very idea of innovation that provided Channel 4 with its initial impetus became a problem for it as the scheduling process became more important in broadcasting. Channel 4 was famous for commissioning only short runs of programmes, and for cancelling programmes, as they put it, 'before they became stale'. There seemed to be too many ideas jostling for a place on television. The innova-tive discussion programme *After Dark* is an example of this tendency. It was cancelled after three seasons, yet the format still returns when an issue like the Gulf War or the death of Diana, Princess of Wales demands it. The result of all this activity of change was that Channel 4's schedule under Jeremy Isaacs seemed very volatile compared to the other channels then broadcasting. It had certain fixed points (news at 7.00pm, *Brookside* at 8.30 etc), but these were comparatively few. This was not untypical of European television in the early 1980s when Channel 4 was founded. The scheduling grid, with its strict time-slots was already a commonplace tool, but scheduling remained a matter of 'fitting in' the programmes that were being provided by the programme-makers. Jeremy Isaacs adopted such an approach in constructing the original Channel 4, by allowing commissioning editors to think about (and even contract for) programmes in all different shapes, sizes and aspirations. Once the process was well underway and the launch date approached, he produced a programming grid at a meeting and asked 'How are we going to fit all this stuff in?'[7]

However, as the era of availability developed, Channel 4's floating schedule became a problem rather than an advantage. Greater viewer choice meant less viewer loyalty, and less viewer loyalty meant that programmes and even schedules became less familiar. Even Jeremy Isaacs sometimes complained that 'people can't find our pro-grammes'. The new chief executive, Michael Grade, a surprise appointment in 1987, felt he had to address this problem. Grade's analysis, born from his experiences in mass entertainment channels in Britain and America, was that familiarity was a key element in a successful television channel. Yet familiarity and Channel 4's remit of experimentation sat uneasily together. Grade's solution was to introduce the idea of stripped schedules: to provide the same kind of programme at the same time on every weekday. In the early evening, he did so with comedy programmes (in competition with BBC and ITV early evening news); between 8.00 and 9.00pm, leisure and education programming; at 10.00pm a major drama series or a film. This strategy was successful; Channel 4's audience increased, but the strategy had several difficult effects. It tied programmes to the length of the slot, eliminating the sometimes wilfully strange programme lengths that had been used in Jeremy Isaac's time, and making more difficult the clearing of the schedules for a special event like *Shoa*. And it made inevitable Channel 4's painful encounter with one of the key facts of modern television: the need for quantity.

Channel 4's schedules began to rely increasingly on imported American programming: the major drama at 10.00pm was more often an American series like *St Elsewhere* or *E.R.* than it was British produced. This was because Channel 4, committed to a programme of feature film financing, had the resources to make only some thirty hours of series drama a year. In addition, there was a natural limit to the amount of series drama that could be repeated from ITV. And the 6.00pm comedy slot was filled by *Roseanne* and *The Cosby Show* more often than by *Desmond's*. These were the 'tent-poles' of Channel 4's schedule, the more popular programmes which might recruit viewers to watch the preceding and subsequent programmes. Channel 4's reliance on the USA for such programming was made more intense by Grade's famous refusal to show subtitled programming (even cinema films) before midnight, and not to countenance dubbed programming at all. By the beginning of the 1990s, Channel 4's reliance on American imports for its most popular programmes began to be a frequent topic of complaint amongst programme-makers and even other broadcasters.

Elsewhere in the schedule, innovative programming began to give way to programming that was designed to shock. This was particularly true of the late night schedules on Friday and Saturday, where Grade's strategy was to court a youth audience that he saw was not being served by other channels. At the Independent Film and Video Department, for instance, Stuart Cosgrove developed the notion of 'zones' of programming, which meant areas of the schedule with a 'keep out' sign attached. His first foray, the *Red Light Zone*, was a late night series focussing on sexuality. Launched amid some highly lurid and controversial publicity, this series of diverse programmes nevertheless contained many interesting moments. But its success set the pattern for a shift from experiment and innovation towards outrage and sleaze, all justified by reference to an underdeveloped and overworked concept of post-modernism. The Zone concept itself was an early example of the increasing tendency of Channel 4 to 'package' individual programmes within an overarching title. Before long, the identity of these 'strands' (as they are known in British television) became increasingly important, with the strand identity prescribing the kinds of approaches that could be used within them.

This was in part the result of Channel 4 adjusting to the new realities of British broadcasting. Multi-channel television had become a reality for about 20 per cent of British homes, and at the same time the level of competition between the established terrestrial channels had become more intense. British television was again looking at the experience of the USA as a cautionary example, seeing the remorseless decline of the networks as their own fate unless they did something to forestall it. So British television launched upon a much more competitive attitude to scheduling which crucially involved the development of recognisable and long-running programme titles. The BBC began to refer to these as 'brands', with all the market values that this implies. Some, even within the BBC, were 'strands', that is recognisable groupings of individual documentaries made under the overall control of a single strand editor. In moving towards the policy of stranding, Michael Grade was merely attempting to ensure that Channel 4 had a continuing place in this new broadcasting environment.

His other problem was the hardening attitude of the Thatcher government. The lingering consensus approach exemplified by William Whitelaw had vanished. In its place stood a seemingly unassailable autocracy, bolstered by military success in the Malvinas and electoral success against a weak and divided Labour Party. Thatcher made occasional forays into the realm of television, and paid attention to those in her party who saw it as 'run by socialists and woolly liberals'. Michael Grade was pilloried in the influential *Daily Mail* newspaper as 'Britain's pornographer-in-chief'.[8] And hanging over Channel 4, as its commercial prospects improved under Grade, was the very real threat of privatization. In this context, it is not surprising that programme-making became more timid. Outspoken documentaries were replaced by 'fly on the wall' documentaries, observing the lives of institutions like the army or the medical profession, or looking at unfortunate individuals in difficult situations. Such documentaries had two advantages: they told a story based on vivid characters, and they promoted no general conclusions about the state of society. This was left up to viewers, if they chose to reach them.

In 1997, Michael Grade suddenly resigned, having successfully fought off all attempts to privatize the channel and set it on a commercially viable course as a self-sufficient and still innovative broadcaster. His successor was Michael Jackson, one of the founding independent producers who had since spent many years at the BBC. His task is to redefine Channel 4's attitude to experiment and innovation. This is not easy to achieve as the options that were open to Jeremy Isaacs are no longer there. Television has changed, and Channel 4 has to find a new role within it. The practices of demand-led broadcasting present particular difficulties. Channel 4 can interpret audience statistics and construct strategies from them, but it has to communicate its needs to a wide constituency of independent producers. Such an act of communication, however, could give away key strategies to competing broadcasters. So increasingly a trusted group of production companies is drawn into a confidential relationship of communication. In the long term, of course, this also has its dangers. Over-dependence on particular companies can lead to creative atrophy or to unacceptable financial demands from those companies.

However this issue is resolved, there remains a greater problem. The question of quantity is crucial and presents particular difficulties for Channel 4. To a significant extent, television is no longer a craft industry, where the self-belief of dedicated individuals in a privileged work situation will ensure that quality programmes are made. With availability comes a multiplication of examples of any one format. What used to be a single documentary will become a four-part series, with each episode taking a slightly different approach to a topic. On average, no more than 10 per cent of the audience will see more than one episode of that series. And programme formats are devised which can endlessly replicate themselves to fill the space available, producing each episode with a slight difference of content within a tightly defined overall format. Such formats can become brands: instantly recognisable to a vast public far larger than the audience for any one episode. This is an industrial context, where a great deal of the work involved seems repetitious and unimportant, if not trivial. Innovation and experiment may well be involved in producing the pilots and early episodes, but, by episode 30 or episode 99, a stream-lined production system will be in place to ensure continuity and standardization. Clearly, this is not the situation in which Channel 4 began. This whole process runs contrary to Channel 4's established practice of short runs and frequent change. Yet at the same time, such a practice of continuous innovation is Channel 4's distinctiveness as a brand.

The hard-won lessons of early Channel 4 programmes are now the givens of British broadcasting. Channel 4 pioneered the creation of programming that refused balance and adopted a diversity of modes of address. Many of the most important features of Channel 4 which enabled it to undertake this task have now become problems for it. The era of availability which it helped to bring in has not been an easy time for Channel 4, and the coming era of plenty will be even less so.

---

[1] For other accounts of the genesis of Channel 4 see Sylvia Harvey, 'Channel 4 Television: from Annan to Grade' in Stuart Hood (ed), *Behind the Screens: The Structure of British Television in the Nineties* (London: Lawrence and Wishart, 1994); Stephen Lambert, *Channel 4: Television with a Difference?* (London: British Film Institute, 1982); Jeremy Isaacs, *Storm Over Four; A Personal Account* (London: Weidenfeld and Nicolson, 1989); and David Docherty, David E. Morrison and Michael Tracey, *Keeping Faith? Channel 4 and its Audience* (London: John Libbey and Company Ltd, 1988).

[2] 'The Annan Report': Home Office, *Report of the Committee on the Future of Broadcasting* (London: HMSO, 1977).

[3] For William Whitelaw's role in the creation of Channel 4, see pp 20-1 of Isaacs: *Storm Over Four.*

[4] Isaacs himself wrote, '[The commissioning editors'] choices would in the end govern what we did. The channel could only be as good as the judgements of those who worked for it.' *Ibid.*, p 34.

[5] As Isaacs wrote, 'I had never doubted, thinking too much television too unthink-ing, too bland, that Channel 4 would broadcast programmes that put, as forcibly as possible, a forcible point of view.' *Ibid.*, p 53. Particularly relevant to the problem of balance in the early years of Channel 4 is Christopher Hird, 'Everything but the truth' in John Wyver (ed), *The Edinburgh International Television Festival 1984* (Edin-burgh: Edinburgh International Television Festival, 1984); and John Ranelagh, 'The anthill (ideas for factual TV)' in Farrukh Dhondy (ed), *Edinburgh International Television Festival '86* (Edinburgh: Edinburgh International Television Festival, 1986).

[6] Isaacs: *Storm Over Four.*

[7] See *City Limits*, 6-12 November 1981, p 82.

[8] Paul Johnson, *Daily Mail*, 4 June 1996.

CHAPTER 11

THE THIRD ERA OF TELEVISION: PLENTY

As television moves into the new millennium, it offers a strange spectacle of uneven development. The industry is rushing towards an emerging era of plenty whilst the majority of viewers are still coming to terms with the era of availability. Television is full of new technologies, new challenges and new uncertainties. At stake is its development away from an economy dominated by terrestrial broadcasting that is free at the point of viewing. That was still the characteristic form of television in the age of availability, which extended television by multiplying channels and filling the empty hours that were typical of the era of scarcity. In many countries, such a service still characterizes the typical experience of television culture for most consumers, yet already within the industry there are those who predict the end of broadcast television. Their vision of the era of plenty consigns the whole process of working through and the practice of public service broadcasting to the dustbin of history. Yet there are persuasive reasons for believing that broadcasting will not wither away. Some can be found within the development of the era of availability itself.

For a significant minority, especially in urban areas, television already offers a whole raft of other services: cable and satellite channels numbered in their tens and even hundreds. Britain launched digital television services in 1998 which offered alongside the existing broadcast and satellite channels a large number of subscription-based channels hitherto available only on cable, plus some entirely new services such as Channel 4's art-house channel FilmFour. In the long run (perhaps 20 years) digital transmission and reception technology will replace the existing analogue system, just as the 625 line signal standard replaced 405 between 1964 and 1980. But at the beginning of the new millennium, British viewers are still faced with a core service of five terrestrial channels and a number of different routes whereby they can access further services at an extra cost. All of these are broadcast channels, and most of them are economically viable because they are supported by subscriptions rather than by advertising and so can address particular audiences. They take two forms: premium services and genre-defined branded services.

Premium services often define themselves, like terrestrial broadcasters, in relation to time, and so their struggles with terrestrial broadcasters have been particularly vivid. Many deal with material whose market value depends on newness: sport and films. A sporting event has maximum value at the moment in which it is being performed, before the outcome is decided. Its value then declines sharply, until it can establish a residual value as a 'classic', an 'historic moment'. Films are no different. They are more valuable the closer they are to their initial newness, the moment of cinema release with its attendant publicity and circulation as a public event in the television talk arenas. They then cascade down a series of 'windows', defined in terms of time, from video rental, to video sale, then first broadcasts on a premium service, then first and subsequent free-to-air broadcasts. Again, if a particular film can establish itself as a classic, it can discover fresh value and pass through this circuit in part or whole again. The strategy of the re-release of *Citizen Kane* in a new print or the director's cut of *Bladerunner* is a demonstration of this process. These films are new again for a new audience, because of age and durability in the case of *Citizen Kane*, and because of a cult status and the fact of a studio version rather than director's version being released originally in the case of *Bladerunner*. Premium services are able to charge sometimes substantial subscriptions and one-off fees.[1] In the era of scarcity, such time-tied events were natural material for broadcasters, and some of the periodization of the schedule was based upon a calendar of such events. This history lies behind the current strategy in Britain of a list of 'reserve events', the

highlights of the sporting year, which are required by the government to be offered to terrestrial broadcasters for live coverage. But
many other sports events are not, and the bidding war for the rights
to show them between broadcasters and premium services has
transformed the economy of many sports by the injection of large
amounts of television money. It has also transformed television, for
sport in the era of scarcity was one of the key elements in providing
a service that was truly universal. Films, too, could have been
overtaken by a similar bidding war, but the strategy of staggered
release windows has proved more lucrative in the long run.

Not all the new multi-channel services are premium ones. Others
offer the same kinds of programming as the universalist broadcast
channels. They have distinctive brand identities based on a single
genre of programming. Discovery deals in nature, wildlife and
outdoor adventure; Sci-Fi in science fiction; FilmFour in edgy films
that tend not to be shown on terrestrial television; Sky Movies in
films before they appear in sell-through video or on the terrestrial
channels; Granada Breeze in lifestyle programming and Men and
Motors in male lifestyle programming; The Cartoon Network in,
well, cartoons. It is as though a fragment of the schedule of a
terrestrial channel had broken off and developed in isolation to fill a
whole channel. The long established pattern for the scheduling of
these channels – apart from those using studio-based magazine
formats – is to repeat a monthly list of programmes in different
timeslots so that they can reach the audiences that are available at
different times of day and night. At its limit, this development has
brought the most surprising results. A channel devoted to the tango,
broadcast by satellite from Argentina, can be received by the hand-
fuls of enthusiasts in European and American cities, but only if they
have a powerful satellite dish or a particularly enlightened cable
service supplier. There are, in other words, many channels and many
surprising choices already available with effort. The era of plenty will
make the taking up of such options easier, if at a price. So the
possible nature of the emerging era can be discerned from the nature
of these new channels. Such channels have not only extended the
choices of those who receive them. They have begun to explore the
nature of that choice in broadcast programming: showing both how
choice may be structured and guided in the era of plenty and also
what its limits might be.

Television and Branding

In the multi-channel environments of the era of availability, the importance of branding has quickly become obvious. This world is full of brands, titles which incarnate not only the essence of the material offered by a channel, but also, as the brand becomes known, its claims to quality. The brand is far more than a logo as Walt Disney realized many years ago. And as Christopher Anderson shows, 'Television served a crucial role in Disney's plans to create an economic and cultural phenomenon that would exceed the boundaries of any single communications medium ... television's figurative representation of Disneyland actually called the amusement park into existence, making it possible for the first time to unite the disparate realms of the Disney empire.'[2] The Disney brand was applied from the 1950s onwards to a whole range of products from toys to theme parks, and is associated with the key characteristics of Walt Disney's films from *Snow White* onwards: the qualities of wholesomeness, child-orientation, homely simplicity of narration, consistent high quality of product, universality of appeal, and a vague and comfortable aura of education. So strong was the brand that Disney's first product, Mickey Mouse, Walt's 'varmint', was forced to shed some of its more mischievous characteristics to conform with it. Now the Disney brand extends quite unproblematically into the market-place of multi-channel television, instantly identifying a kind of television. Similarly, National Geographic applies its existing brand to a television channel. MTV has created a brand in this new market-place, a brand that it can now apply to other products. In the 1990s, too, the major terrestrial and even public service broadcasters began to discover their nature as key brands. Every channel has an identity, diffuse though it may currently be for some generalist terrestrial broadcasters.

For instance, Britain's ITV, constituted out of a coalition of companies, has a very vague brand identity compared to that of a focused cable channel like Discovery. It is not even sure of its brand name, having flirted with rebranding as 'Channel 3'. A BBC exercise in brand definition in 1995 could at least come up with the concepts 'Our BBC1' and 'My BBC2' which encapsulated the concept of public proprietorship combined with shared or more individual interests. However even this early exercise in brand definition had its problems. For example, it omitted the more experimental nature of some BBC2 output (which many people spontaneously attribute to Channel 4 anyway), concentrating on the 'specialist interest' aspect: preferring Jeremy Clarkson over Armando Ianucci. Nevertheless, the BBC's identity is clear compared to that of the ITV and this clarity is part of the recognition by the world's remaining public service broadcasters that some of their basic values are vital and valuable 'brands' in an increasingly competitive market. After years of self-deprecation in the face of commercial onslaughts of various kinds, they now discover that their record and history actually counts for something important. Their brand identity lies in the overall character of programmes, their placing in a recognised pattern incarnating both viewing habits and judgements of 'fitness for audience purpose'. The brand of all generalist channels, in other words, lies in the schedule and how that schedule is known by their client audiences. As *Variety* recently remarked: 'Broadcasters are becoming niche-casters, and when they don't serve their niche, they suffer. The most drastic example this season is the CBS Friday line-up, an attempt to steal ABC's TGIF [Thank Goodness It's Friday, i.e. release from work to leisure] audience of young moms and kids. While CBS has lowered its median age on the night by four years, its largest Friday night audience remains the over 50 year olds.'[3] Despite CBS's changes to its programming, in other words, the channel brand image generated by an address to an older audience on Fridays still dominated network viewing habits.

Brands exist at other levels in broadcasting and entertainment as well. Long-running programmes or successful films can also become brands, and are often referred to as 'sub-brands' to distinguish them from the brand identities of the channels on which they might appear. In this case, the brand consists of a known storyline or scenario, a fantasy with particular elements that can be successfully repeated through a number of different forms. The process is well established in relation to the cinema. The French film *La Femme Nikita* is remade in an American version which then is remade into a long-running television series. The film *L.A. Confidential* is used as the basis for a TV series which is set several years before the events in the film. The children's animated series *Ghostbusters* was created from the 1984 film of the same name, and enjoyed such a success that the sequel film *Ghostbusters II* was made five years after the first. The film *Men in Black* reappears as a computer game; and the computer game *Tomb Raider* reappears as a film. At each stage, subsidiary forms of merchandising are created as well: lunchboxes, clothing with logos, novelizations etc. The term usually applied to this process, the 'spinoff', is increasingly inappropriate as the process becomes more established and pre-planned. The operation of the fiction-as-brand is the creation of fresh products using an existing and recognised brand name and associated logo. It will be an important component in the entertainment industry of the future. What used to be spinoffs are now capable of yielding more profit than the product that originally created the brand; indeed, the original product is often designed expressly to produce the possibility of its onward exploitation as a brand. From the consumers' point of view, a brand offers a known and repeatable set of pleasures, a fantasy that can be indulged through different manifestations and a set of values that can be explored over and over again. In the era of availability, American entertainment cinema was the main brand-creating machine in entertainment. Film characters and scenarios regularly fuelled productions in other media, from cartoon strips to books and television. The process gradually became evident in the television industry as well, and stretched beyond fiction.

Any long-running television format is, in essence, a brand: the title identifies a reliable set of characteristics of consistent quality. In a crowded media environment, the value of such a brand increases as it cuts through problems of consumer recognition. So elements of a successful brand can be applied to new products, as seen in the creation of new series using actors whose roles have been established elsewhere. The creation of the series *Frasier* around the character of Dr Frasier Crane from *Cheers* was an early example. The BBC has experimented with creating drama vehicles around characters from its soap operas, as with Michele Collins who played Cindy Beale in the soap *EastEnders* incarnating what is essentially the same character in *Sunburn*, a series whose subject derives from a successful documentary soap about the travel industry. Similarly, *Casualty*, the long-running hospital emergency room drama, has spawned *Holby City*, based in the surgical wards of the same fictional hospital and even sharing some of *Casualty*'s main characters in subsidiary parts.

The strengths and difficulties of the process are well illustrated by two brands: the cookery expert Delia Smith and children's animation series *Thomas the Tank Engine*. Neither has any claim to aesthetic merit, and in both cases, the making of television programmes is a rather incidental moment in a much larger process. What matters is the broadcasting of those programmes. Broadcasting rather than programme-making is what creates brands. Delia Smith's appeal lies in her lack of flamboyance and her accessible appealing recipes. She speaks with a flat estuary English accent and her presentation is rather characterless and down-to-earth. In a television universe filled with chefs increasingly concerned with style and self-promotion rather than the substance of food, Delia Smith was the only person able to present a series entitled *How to Cook*. In book form, this topped the Christmas 1998 best-seller charts. Delia Smith is a brand: her endorsement of products and supermarkets earns her and the BBC large amounts of money. Her sudden enthusiasm for cranberries promoted these exotic North American berries to the centre of many British dining tables, through a close link with the Sainsbury's supermarket chain. Yet the Delia Smith television programmes are simplicity themselves. They deal in the small change of witness, seeing food being made. The only production challenges come from the cantankerousness of the food itself. An omelette at 2.15 is perfect, but an omelette at 2.18 is a piece of leather, and no amount of coaxing can reverse the process for a second take or a close-up. Production logistics have to plan to deal with this simple fact, and everything else tends to be a routine matter.

Series like Delia Smith's *How To Cook* may be cheap and unchallenging to make, but they use the cultural position of broadcast television to create valuable brands. The children's series *Thomas the Tank Engine* shows how far this can go. Taking an innocuous series of children's books from the 1950s and 1960s, Britt Alcroft planned the creation of a brand and used television to promote it. A simple series of animated children's programmes, narrated by Ringo Starr, was created and on broadcast a large range of toys and other merchandising was available. The result was a safe range of gifts for the very young, trading in part on their parents' and grandparents' memories of the original books. Thomas the Tank Engine became a brand, much to the bemusement of his creator the Rev. Awdry. Such initiatives created huge problems for the public service ethos of the BBC as well. The Controller of BBC Children's Television for many years, Anna Home, used to boast about the games of cat-and-mouse she played with the manufacturers and retailers of merchandising that linked to children's programming. By withholding the broadcast date of a merchandising-linked series until the last moment, she hoped that the BBC would not be seen as a party to the financial exploitation of children's tastes. Nowadays, this is an accepted part of BBC cultural activity, and the Corporation has bought the Noddy brand (derived from Enid Blyton's children's books) and shares in

the income from Tellytubby toys. The incorporation of such lucrative brand exploitation, which relies on the cultural position of public
service broadcasting, has been a long and difficult debate within the
BBC, and is still not resolved. Yet it is becoming more crucial
because branding brings an element of reassurance into the increasingly complicated choices that viewers will have to make.

Time Famine and Choice Fatigue

Brands guide choice, and the era of plenty is conceived as being a
time of almost infinite choice. Televisions will be equipped with a
greater number of peripheral devices which will enable them to
process more information and to play an important role as domestic
information systems. With digital services comes the electronic
programme guide, which is operated by a remote control but can
also be used for home shopping activities. A further development is
a keyboard which can use the same infra-red sensor system as the
remote control. This allows a far easier means of accessing and
inputting information than the conventional remote control which is
limited to numbers only. This opens the possibility of quick access to
teletext pages, the use of the television as an e-mail system, and the
ubiquitous idea of home shopping, or e-commerce to give its
fashionable name. Many of these developments have nothing to do
with broadcast television as a social form apart from sharing its
screen. But for television as a business activity, it is clearly important
that forms of e-commerce could be accessed from television programmes, and that broadcasting clearly has a future as a point of
entry to informational universes.

The era of plenty will also bring a qualitative change in the nature
of broadcast television itself. Electronic programme guides will
enable viewers to ignore channel schedules and seek the particular
kinds of programming that they crave from a menu of several
hundred channels. This technology will enable television consumers
to select from the many programmes available at any one time by
groupings of genre, actor and personality, language and many other
parameters. It will also offer choices based on the evidence of
previous preferences. The flexible and adaptable electronic programme guide is often seen as a liberation from the tyranny that the

schedules seem to exercise over the vagaries of real life. Clearly the ability to access weather forecasts when you want rather than when the broadcasters want to show them will be useful. But the real question is whether this increased and tailored choice will bring a profound transformation – or even disappearance – of the broadcast form of television, or will they develop as yet unused potentials in television technology? Clues can be found by examining two areas: consumer choice and the relationship between broadcasting and time.

Choice is complicated, and brings its own uncertainties. Within the home, where television is consumed, the diffuse anxiety brought on by the experience of the world beyond the home is if anything intensified. Since the private household is the privileged site of consumption, all the anxieties that hover around consumer choice are expressed in the home. To choose is to be aware of alternative possibilities, possibilities that are being missed. So a feeling of anxiety results, that of 'time famine', the feeling of having too much to do and not enough time to fit it into. Time itself has become a commodity, but, despite various science fiction fantasies, any individual has only a finite amount of time at their disposal. But no-one knows how much of this crucial resource they actually will have. This is one of the great underlying uncertainties of contemporary consumer existence. The existential difficulty of today's consumer is this lurking sense of mortality whilst being confronted by many attractive options, be they television programmes or leisure activities, commodities or ideas. One aspect of the experience of time famine is the partial paralysis of choice: the hesitation between possibilities all of which seem equally attractive, in the knowledge that no time exists to savour them all.

Time famine therefore produces the feeling of juggling options. The act of choice itself consumes time ('takes time' as we say). And the consequences of choices leave most urban individuals with too much to do. So traditional ways of dividing time into set patterns have been eroded. Instead of meal times, there is the phenomenon of 'grazing'. Instead of time patterns of broadcasting, there are personal attempts to escape them with the use of time-shift video recording and the call for video on demand. There is a tendency towards desynchronization of activities in the modern world, and particularly in the modern home. Individuals grab the opportunity to do things when they can, or when they feel it is most convenient. We no longer have 'spare time', we no longer have to 'kill time' and feel very uneasy at 'wasting time'. Time famine breeds impatience, and the desire that choices should be immediately available. 'Convenience' and 'on demand' are seductive words to the choice-obsessed time famine victim. The developments that are producing television's age of plenty respond to those requirements. Yet in reducing the patterns of everyday life and replacing them by a constantly wide horizon of choice, this desynchronization seems to be increasing the level of anxiety rather than reducing it. Stripping away pattern and habit opens up tempting vistas of choice and convenience, yet it intensifies time famine and the feelings surrounding it.

In such circumstances, choice fatigue emerges. This is the feeling that choices are simply too difficult; a nostalgia for pattern, habit and an era when choices seemed few. Choice fatigue is a combination of impatience, a great modern vice, and the sense of simply not wanting to be bothered. Choice fatigue is the experience of the customer who feels an urgent need for a cup of coffee, but is confronted instead by multiple choices which have to be negotiated: choice of bean, of brew, of configuration of milk, of various additives and subtractives. Choice fatigue produces the response 'Why can't you just give me a cup of coffee?' There are moments when choice is an imposition rather than a freedom. Broadcast television answers to this feeling. From the perspective of choice fatigue, its schedules might appear to be liberating. They take away the crushing burden of having to make a selection by offering a pattern in which there is just one option (this programme at this time only) or a manageable range of choices between clearly defined, known quantities (the pattern of the terrestrial broadcast schedule).

The Possibilities of Choice

These problems are not unique to television, of course. They show that television is yet again mutating in its own particular way according to developments in the wider consumer market. The increasing segmentation of markets and multiplication of choices was a tendency that began in television's age of availability. Now the consumer market in styles has become a vast web of possibilities and throws up its own internal problem. How is it possible to plan production and distribution of goods when so many variants are in play? The economics of the small production run and last minute supply can answer this up to a point. But the major retailers, especially supermarkets, are now looking towards a further sophistication in the prediction and management of choice. They combine the technologies of electronic check-outs, which record every purchase, with the system of loyalty cards which give customers small rebates on the overall value of their purchases. So each purchaser's patterns of preferences can be identified and charted over a long period. Or at least, that is the aim, since the ability to process the raw data that has already been collected is still too expensive to be economically viable for a few years.

The aim of such an undertaking is not yet entirely clear. Is it to produce more targeted marketing, to offer Italianate products to those who seem to prefer Italian cuisine, or coupons only to coupon-clippers, in the same way that an electronic programme guide will offer tonight's news or wildlife programmes to someone who seems to have preferred them in the past? If so, just like the electronic programme guide, they will soon run up against the vagaries of household power structures as well as the consumer's resentment that choices are being closed off without an explicit decision on their part. Or is it to reduce the plethora of choices to predictable patterns, segmenting the market in the same way that BARB figures produce a segmented mapping of television audiences? In that case, the huge mass of supermarket checkout data will have produced rather meagre and problematic results. Or is this part of a long term strategy of replacing the ritual of the weekly shop for basic domestic goods with e-commerce? In this perspective the supermarket data could analyse domestic purchases, producing a list of options sent to a domestic terminal (perhaps the TV set itself) to be accepted or rejected according to whether there is enough cat food or detergent in the house for the moment. The whole transaction could done electronically for later automatic delivery. The unappealing act of wheeling shopping trolleys full of basic goods would become a thing of the past. Shopping would take on a new identity: no longer a chore but the sensual pleasure of browsing through a myriad of exotic purchase options. Supermarket shelves would be stacked with dreams rather than baked beans. Such is the dream of retailing's planners, and it is shared by many in the television industry.

Both television and supermarkets provide the staples of modern domestic existence, and the television industry is fond of making the parallel explicit. This vision of an interactive tailored provision is no exception. Interactive television has thrown up many possibilities. One is the idea of audience participation in the creation of programmes, choosing the next plot development in a soap opera, for example. This is unlikely to work because of the mechanisms of story-telling, which rest on the surprise of plot moves provided by the narration, no matter how predictable they might seem in retrospect or even as the story unrolls. However, different possibilities do seem to have more potential. Comedy shows are now developing associated websites in which fans can write their own material, taking on the guise of their favourite characters as a fulfilling extension of the fantasy into a new medium. The infrared keyboard would simply integrate this with television viewing. Another possibility is the 'tell me more' function. A factual magazine programme like *Watchdog Healthcheck* might run a five-minute item about a condition like Asperger's Syndrome, and the interactive programme guide could provide access to the last ten items on that or similar subjects, downloaded from a central archival database. This is an extension of the use of teletext backup information, but requires formidable computing memory, processing and transmission infrastructures that will require huge investment. That investment is probable because the logic of such a development leads to the next step: if a viewer can recall wanted information, why not reorder the contents of the programme in the first place to provide only those items that will be of interest. Interactive television would allow a viewer to build their own *Watchdog Healthcheck* from items only about surgery, or the over-45s, or food safety. In factual rather than fiction programming, interactivity would seem to have a promising future.

However, it will not replace the conventional use of broadcast television. During the era of availability, early evening factual magazines like the BBC's *Watchdog* brand have developed a genre of infotainment in which the style of the programme and the figures of the presenters matter almost as much as the information that is conveyed. They appeal to a different viewing attitude: the browser rather than the tell-me-more. As such, they belong within a powerfully inclusive broadcasting culture of working through, where the ostensible information conveyed may not be the real interest of the programme at all. Only one step away from *Watchdog Healthcheck* lies the phenomenally successful leisure format *Changing Rooms*, in which neighbours assisted by professionals redecorate a room in each other's houses. The informational content would appear to be firmly

in the area of 'how to redecorate', but the themes worked through by
the programme are very different. The appeal of the programme lies
in its address to questions of class and taste, style and appearance.
This takes place across a powerful emotional dynamic, involving an
insight into the nature of the relationships of the two couples, with
their neighbours and even with the professional designers who
behave with a degree of pantomime exaggeration. Infotainment of
this kind resists interactivity, or at the very least it demonstrates that
broadcast television is distinct from an information driven system.
However, at the same time, leisure and other infotainment formats
can offer a powerful gateway to interactive information systems,
through the ability to call up related material. This could be other
related programmes held in a searchable archive, or it could be
reversioned material from the programme itself. Anyone interested
in the decorating techniques used in *Changing Rooms* would be able to
call up material detailing that technique, material that was shot
during the production but not used in the final broadcast programme. Interactivity is therefore likely to produce new forms of
audiovisual material, and it will begin to stretch broadcasting rather
than replace it. This is not television as we know it or use it: it has
nothing to do with working through. It will be a genuinely new
development, a convergence with other ways of working with
information.

The traditional forms of broadcasting answer the feelings of time
famine and choice fatigue by enabling or suspending choice. Broadcast schedules present a recognisable fait accompli of choosing and a
known economy of time. In the new environment, broadcasting will
also provide the possibility of choice, acting as a potential gateway to
interactive media and searchable archives. Broadcasting has a
valuable stock of brands that will make it a powerful ally in this
process, and its continuing wide reach across the population will
enable it to continue to create and sustain those brands for many
years to come. However, most of these brands lie in the more
routine or mundane areas of programme-making like *How to Cook,* as
well as in the contemporary forms of witness offered by reality-based
programmes of all kinds. The more high profile and high cost genres
of drama and special event programming will tend to disappear to
subscription-based services, and the free-to-air broadcasters would
have to seek them (if they wanted them) through forms of co-
production ventures with those channels. The implication of the era
of plenty is clearly that broadcasting will intensify its move towards

the production of multiple part and open-ended forms. This tendency has already caused problems for Channel 4, as the previous chapter has demonstrated. The pressures of the era of plenty are likely to intensify the everydayness of broadcast television's sense of witness.

Yet at the same time, the new forms of information-driven television, the subscription channels and the searchable databases, will tend to bring back the definitive kinds of programme-making that characterized the era of scarcity but tended to disappear with it. There would be a clear informational market value in new versions of the BBC blockbusters of the 1960s like Kenneth Clark's *Civilisation* or Jacob Bronowski's *The Ascent of Man* or even series which, in the age of availability, were driven into the fringes of broadcasting like American PBS's *The Civil War* from the 1990s. But these would appear in a distinctive form, where the linear argument of a modern (or perhaps 'post-modern') Clark or Bronowski would provide simply a route of access to searchable information, and so would find its own presuppositions more ruthlessly interrogated than was possible in the era of televisual scarcity. Their linear form could well provide a valuable input to the terrestrial broadcast channels, acting both as a traditional public service form and as a marketing device for the searchable informational form.

The Future of Broadcasting and Public Service

All of this is speculation, but necessary speculation. The predictions of the death of broadcast television are every bit as loud now as were those of the end of cinema in the face of competition from television. Now that we understand the differences and the points of mutual interaction between television and cinema, such predictions seem quaint and wrong-headed. Yet many rash and irreversible business decisions were taken at the time on the basis of these predictions, the neglect and destruction of far too many of Britain's cinemas being one of them. Rather than investing in modern multi-screen complexes, the companies controlling British exhibition liquidated their investments by selling off their prime properties for other uses. The result was not only a further decline in cinema attendance but the destruction of a filmgoing culture in many towns and cities. The same kinds of decisions may well be taken in relation to British television, and particularly the future of public service broadcasting and the licence fee, if the more extreme predictions are taken seriously.

Broadcast television will continue as a distinctive form of television. No longer will it have to undertake rather inappropriate tasks as it did in the era of scarcity: the showing of routine sports events for example. Broadcast television has developed a vital social role. In the era of scarcity, it carved out a domestic niche, and in the era of availability it developed its role as a forum for working through social pressures as well as sharing social pleasures. Both these roles have new relevance in the emerging era of plenty. Television's easy domesticity, for which it paid a high price, now addresses that moment of relaxation away from the tensions of choice fatigue and time famine: that moment when 'you turn on the TV to see what's on'. Broadcast television is distinct in its everydayness and its sense of co-presence with its audience. This is why the viewer behaviour discovered by ethnomethodological studies is so immensely diverse when compared to the profiles generated by statistical audience research. Broadcast television connects with the private and the disconnected moments of individuals, with diffuse feelings of escape and distraction from the adventures of modern consumerism and life in the company of other consumers. This is one of the reasons why television's liveness still matters in a period when the overwhelming majority of televisual experiences on offer have been recorded. Broadcast television, as I have tried to explore in this book, performs an almost therapeutic role for those whose temporary experience of their existence is that of choice fatigue and time famine. As a result it is able to work through the experiences of witness and the epiphenomena of society, both of which induce such feelings.

The other core aspect of broadcast television lies in its ability to provide a voluntary point of social cohesion, of being-together while being-apart. Most of the models of interactivity and choice imply a lone consumer, making choices in isolation. The limited arena of television's scheduling provides the basis on which households can negotiate more collective choices. Yet even for the most isolated viewer, broadcast television's sense of being-together is the basis of working through, the open process of turning over social meanings which has become such a feature of the everyday programming of the age of availability, from daytime talk to infotainment to docu-soaps. This essentially casual process, encountered by any one viewer in a fragmentary way, is a use of television that is utterly distinct from an interactive process dependent on expressions of viewer choice. It answers to the needs to be told a story, to be surprised, rather than the need to find out. Working through is a collective process of making sense of the modern world that uses the linearity of the broadcast medium. It depends upon the universal availability of public service broadcast television services.

Broadcast television established its universality by being free at the point of viewing. There is no specific charge, apart from an annual licence fee where that exists, for viewing television. The costs of commercials are well hidden in other transactions. The age of plenty will be characterized by a development away from this principle. For the television companies, it will be an age of plenty in terms of income streams; for viewers, it will be an age of plenty in terms of charges and subscriptions. To put it bluntly, as some executives have done, they want us to pay more for our television. This is a tremendous gamble on the part of the television industry. At the close of the twentieth century, the industry has embarked on a massive expansion of services without a massive increase in its income. The hope is that television consumers will respond to the offer of more choice, convenience of access, and interactive possibilities by paying increased subscriptions for those services. This risky commercial project will determine the face of television's era of plenty, and, to a significant degree, whether there is an era of plenty at all. It is also a tremendous irony. The price of most goods falls when scarcity gives way to plenty. But not so television: here plenty seems to imply an increase in the costs to the consumer. Perhaps this counter-market logic is the final proof that television programmes are not simple commodities to be compared with baked beans, but have a defining cultural dimension. Even those far-seeing individuals who predicted the era of plenty even whilst the era of availability was still opening, have now backed away from their initial sense that all television would have to be subscription-based.

The process of working through implies that the terrestrial broadcasters of universally available services are the guardians of an open process through which social cohesion can be negotiated. The era of plenty will need such forums as a core service that is universal, free at the point of viewing and has a schedule based on diversity. This is public service television for the new era. The creation of brands on these services and their use to provide gateways to interactive services are the necessary consequence of that key social position. As such, the brands can provide income which can support the provision of such universalist services, but they cannot replace a form of funding that is appropriate for the social role of such services. This will remain the licence fee or its equivalent, which recognises the distinctiveness of broadcasting as a particular form of television which has a separate social function from the interactive and subscription forms of television. The fact that these forms are being launched by broadcasting companies, using brands derived from broadcasting, does not detract from the fundamental point that there should be a public service broadcasting sector that is universal and free at the moment of access. Television companies are diversifying, but the problems that they have in this process should not blind them to the distinctiveness of their current 'core business' in broadcasting. For the era of plenty will not see the end of broadcasting. Broadcasting will cease to be the only or even the predominant form for the consumption of audio-visual matter. Broadcasting will become one distinct form of the audio-visual. It will be distinguished by its continuing, crucial, social role of working through the emotions provoked by the process of witness.

---

[1] The single fee for a special event is well established in relation to one-off sports events like boxing matches. The principle can easily be extended to mix pay-per-view with a basic subscription.

[2] Christopher Anderson, *Hollywood Television: The Studio System in the Fifties* (Austin: University of Texas Press, 1994), pp 134-5.

[3] *Variety*, 20 October 1997.

BIBLIOGRAPHY

Adorno, T., *The Culture Industry*, ed J.M. Bernstein (London: Routledge, 1991)

Aldgate, Anthony and Jeffrey Richards, *Britain Can Take It: The British Cinema in the Second World War* (Oxford: Basil Blackwell, 1986)

Allen, Robert C., *Speaking of Soap Operas* (Chapel Hill/London: University of North Carolina Press, 1985)

—— (ed), *To Be Continued: Soap Operas Around the World* (London: Routledge, 1995).

Altman, Rick (ed), *Sound Theory, Sound Practice* (London: Routledge, 1992)

Anderson, Benedict, *Imagined Communities* (London: Verso, 1983)

Anderson, Christopher, *Hollywood Television: The Studio System in the Fifties* (Austin: University of Texas Press, 1994)

Ang, Ien, *Watching Dallas: Soap Opera and the Melodramatic Imagination* (London: Methuen, 1985)

—— *Desperately Seeking the Audience* (London: Routledge, 1991)

—— *Living Room Wars* (London: Routledge, 1996)

Baehr, Helen and Gillian Dyer (eds), *Boxed In: Women and Television* (London: Pandora Press, 1987)

Bakhtin, Mikhael, *The Bakhtin Reader* (London: Edward Arnold, 1994)

Barthes, Roland, *Image, Music, Text*, trans S. Heath (London: Fontana, 1980)

—— *Camera Lucida, Reflection on Photography* (London: Cape, 1981)

Baudrillard, Jean, *Selected Writings*, ed M. Poster (Stanford: Stanford University Press, 1988)

Bauman, Zygmunt, *Modernity and Ambivalence* (Oxford: Polity Press, 1991)

—— *Postmodern Ethics* (Oxford: Basil Blackwell, 1993)

Bazin, André, *Qu'est-ce que le cinéma?* vol 4 (Paris: Editions du Cerf, 1962)

BBC Corporate Affairs, *Extending Choice* (London: BBC, 1992)

Benjamin, Walter, *Illuminations* (London: Fontana, 1970)

Bennett, Tony, Colin Mercer and Janet Woollacott (eds), *Popular Culture and Social Relations* (Milton Keynes: Open University Press, 1986)

Berman, Marshall, *All That Is Solid Melts into Air* (New York: Simon & Schuster, 1982)

Bhabha, Homi K., *The Location of Culture* (London: Routledge 1994)

Bobo, Francesco and Ib Bonderbjerg, *Nordic Television: History, Politics, Aesthetics* (Copenhagen: Sekvens/University of Copenhagen, 1994)

Boddy, William, *Fifties Television: The Industry and its Critics* (Urbana: University of Illinois Press, 1990)

Bordwell, David, *Narration in the Fiction Film* (London: Methuen, 1985)

Bordwell, David, *et al.*, *The Classical Hollywood Cinema* (London: Routledge, 1988)

Bourdieu, Pierre, *Distinction: A Social Critique of the Judgment of Taste*, trans R. Nice (Cambridge: Harvard University Press, 1984)

Briggs, Asa, *The BBC: The First Fifty Years* (Oxford: Oxford University Press, 1985)

Browne, Nick, 'The political economy of the television (super) text', *Quarterly Review of Film Studies* 9/3 (1984)

Brownlow, Kevin, *The Parade's Gone By* (London: Secker & Warburg, 1968)

Brunsdon, Charlotte, 'Crossroads: Notes on a soap opera', *Screen* 22/4 (1981)

—— 'Satellite dishes and the landscapes of taste', *New Formations* 15 (1991), pp 23-42

Brunsdon, Charlotte, Juliet D'Acci and Lynn Spigel, *Feminist Television Criticism: A Reader* (Oxford: Oxford University Press, 1997)

Carey, John, *Communication as Culture* (London: Unwin Hyman, 1989)

—— *The Intellectuals and the Masses: Pride and Prejudice among the Literary Intelligentsia 1880-1939* (London: Faber and Faber, 1992)

Cassata, Mary and T. Skill (eds), *Life on Daytime Television: Tuning-In American Serial Drama* (Norwood, New Jersey: Ablex Publishing Corporation, 1983)

Castels, Manuel, *The Information Age: Economy, Society and Culture* (Oxford: Basil Blackwell, 1996)

Caudwell, John T., *Televisuality: Style, Crisis and Authority in American Television* (Piscataway, New Jersey: Rutgers University Press, 1995)

Caughie, John, 'Adorno's reproach: repetition, difference and television genre', *Screen* 32/2 (Summer 1991)

Chanan, Michael, *The Dream That Kicks: The Prehistory and Early Years of Cinema in Britain* (London: Routledge, 1982)

—— *Repeated Takes: A Short History of Recording and its Effects on Music* (London: Verso, 1995)

Collett, Peter and R. Lamb, *Watching People Watching Television* (London: Independent Broadcasting Authority, 1986)

Corner, John (ed), *Popular Television in Britain: Studies in Cultural History* (London: British Film Institute, 1991)

—— 'Presumption as theory: realism in television studies', *Screen* 33/1 (Spring 1992)

—— *Television Form and Public Address* (London: Edward Arnold, 1995)

—— *The Art of Record: A Critical Introduction to the Documentary* (Manchester: University of Manchester Press, 1996)

Coward, Rosalind, *Female Desire: Women's Sexuality Today* (London: Paladin, 1984)

—— *Sacred Cows* (London: HarperCollins, 1999)

Coward, Rosalind and John Ellis, *Language and Materialism* (London: Routledge, 1977)

Crisell, Andrew, *An Introductory History of British Broadcasting* (London: Routledge, 1997)

Culler, Jonathan, *On Deconstruction* (London: Routledge, 1983)

Cumberbatch, Guy and D. Howitt, *A Measure of Uncertainty: The Effects of Mass Media* (London: John Libbey and Company Ltd, 1989)

Curran *et al.* (eds), *Impacts and Influences: Essays on Media Power in the Twentieth Century* (London: Methuen, 1987)

Dahlgren, Peter and Colin Sparks (eds), *Communication and Citizenship* (London: Routledge, 1991)

Dayan, Daniel and Elihu Katz, *Media Events: The Live Broadcasting of History* (Cambridge: Harvard University Press, 1992)

De Certeau, Michel, *The Practice of Everyday Life*, trans S. Randall (Bloomington: Indiana University Press, 1984)

De Lauretis, Teresa, *Technologies of Gender* (Bloomington: Indiana University Press, 1987)

Delandes, Jacques and Jacques Richard, *Histoire comparée du cinéma*, vol 2 (Tournai: Editions Casterman, 1968)

Docherty, David, David E. Morrison and Michael Tracey, *Keeping Faith? Channel 4 and its Audience* (London: John Libbey and Company Ltd, 1988)

Dovey, John (ed), *Fractal Dreams* (London: Lawrence and Wishart, 1995)

Dowmunt, Tony (ed), *Channels of Resistance* (London: British Film Institute, 1993)

Dyer, Richard (ed), *Coronation Street* (London: BFI Publishing, 1981)

Ellis, John, *Visible Fictions: Cinema, Television, Video* (London: Routledge, 1982)

Elsaesser, Thomas and Kay Hoffman (eds), *Cinema Futures: Cain, Abel or Cable?* (Amsterdam: University of Amsterdam Press, 1998)

Featherstone, Mike (ed), *Consumer Culture and Postmodernism* (London: Sage, 1990)

Fell, John L. (ed), *Film Before Griffith* (Berkeley: University of California Press, 1983)

Feuer, Jane, Paul Kerr and Tise Vahimagi, *MTM: Quality Television* (London: British Film Institute, 1984)

Fiske, John, *Television Culture* (London: Methuen, 1987)

—— *Remote Control: Television Audiences and Cultural Power* (London: Routledge, 1989)

—— *Power Plays/Power Works* (London: Verso, 1993)

Freud, Sigmund, 'Remembering, repeating and working-through' (1914) in *Standard Edition of the Complete Psychological Works*, vol XII, ed James Strachey (London: Hogarth Press, 1958), p 155

—— *Jokes and their Relation to the Unconscious* (London: Routledge & Kegan Paul, 1966)

Gauntlett, David, *Moving Experiences: Understanding Television's Influences and Effects* (London: John Libbey and Company Ltd, 1995)

Geertz, Clifford, *Local Knowledge* (New York: Basic Books, 1983)

Gellner, Ernest, *Nations and Nationalism* (Oxford: Basil Blackwell, 1983)

Geraghty, Christine, *Women and Soap Opera: A Study of Prime Time Soaps* (Cambridge: Polity Press, 1990)

Geraghty, Christine and David Lusted (eds), *The Television Studies Book* (London: Edward Arnold, 1998)

Gilroy, Paul, *The Black Atlantic* (London: Verso, 1993)

Gitlin, Todd, *Inside Prime Time* (London: Routledge, 1994)

Gledhill, Christine, *Home is Where the Heart Is* (London: British Film Institute, 1987)

Gomery, Douglas, *Movie History: A Survey* (Belmont, California: Wadsworth, 1991)

Goodwin, Andrew and Gary Whannel (eds), *Understanding Television* (London: Routledge, 1990)

Gramsci, Antonio, *Letters From Prison* (London: Cape, 1975)

Gray, Ann, *Video Playtime: The Gendering of a Leisure Technology* (London: Routledge, 1992)

Gray, Frank (ed), *The Hove Pioneers and the Arrival of Cinema* (Brighton: University of Brighton, 1996)

Gregory, Jeanne and Sue Lees, *Policing Sexual Assault* (London: Routledge, 1999)

Gripsrud, Jostein, *The Dynasty Years: Hollywood Television and Critical Media Studies* (London: Routledge, 1995)

—— (ed), *Television and Common Knowledge* (London: Routledge, 1999)

Grote, D., *The End of Comedy: The Sitcom and the Comedic Tradition* (Hamden, Connecticut: Shoe String Press, 1983)

Hampton, Benjamin, *History of the American Film Industry* (Mineola, New York: Dover Publications, 1970)

Hansen, Miriam, *Babel and Babylon: Spectatorship in American Silent Film* (Cambridge: Harvard University Press, 1991)

Hardy, Forsyth (ed), *Grierson on Documentary* (London, Faber and Faber, 1979)

Harvey, David, *The Condition of Postmodernity* (Oxford: Basil Blackwell, 1989)

Heath, Stephen, *Questions of Cinema* (Bloomington: Indiana University Press, 1981)

Heath, Stephen and Gillian Skirrow, 'Television: a world in action', *Screen* 18/2 (1977)

Hebdige, Dick, *Hiding in the Light* (London: Routledge, 1988)

Hendricks, Gordon, *Eadweard Muybridge* (New York: Grossman, 1975)

Higson, Andrew, *Waving the Flag* (Oxford: Oxford University Press, 1995)

Hobsbawm, Eric, *Age of Extremes: The Short Twentieth Century 1914-1991* (London: Michael Joseph, 1994)

Home Office, *Report of the Committee on the Future of Broadcasting* (London: HMSO, 1977)

Hood, Stuart (ed), *Behind the Screens: The Structure of British Television in the Nineties* (London: Lawrence and Wishart, 1994)

Houston, Beverle, 'Viewing television: the metapsychology of endless consumption', *Quarterly Review of Film Studies* 9/3 (1984)

Hughes, Robert, *The Culture of Complaint: The Fraying of America* (Oxford: Oxford University Press, 1993)

Humphreys, Patrick, *Mass Media and Media Policy in Western Europe* (Manchester: Manchester University Press, 1996)

Isaacs, Jeremy, *Storm Over Four: A Personal Account* (London: Weidenfield & Nicolson, 1989)

Jameson, Frederick, *Postmodernism, or the Cultural Logic of Late Capitalism* (London: Verso, 1991)

Jenkins, H., *Textual Poachers: Television Fans and Participatory Culture* (London: Routledge, 1992)

Jensen, Klaus Bruhn and Karin E. Rosengren, 'Five traditions in search of an audience', *European Journal of Communications* 5/3-4 (1990)

Jhally, Stephen and Justin Lewis, *Enlightened Racism: The Cosby Show, Audiences and the Myth of the American Dream* (Boulder: Westview Press, 1992)

Katz, Ephraim, *Macmillan International Film Encyclopedia* (London: Harper-Collins, 1998)

Keighron, Peter, 'Video diaries: what's up doc?', *Sight and Sound* 3/10 (October 1998)

King, John, *Magical Reels: A History of Cinema in Latin America* (London: Verso, 1990)

Kuhn, Annette (ed), *Screen Histories* (Oxford: J. Stacey, 1998)

Lambert, Stephen, *Channel 4: Television with a Difference?* (London: British Film Institute, 1982)

Lash, Stephen and J. Urry, *Economies of Sign and Space* (London: Sage, 1994)

Lewis, Justin, *The Ideological Octopus* (London: Routledge, 1991)

Leyda, Jay, *Kino* (London: Allen & Unwin, 1983)

Livingstone, Sonia M., *Making Sense of Television: The Psychology of Audience Interpretation* (Oxford: Pergamon, 1990)

Livingstone, Sonia M. and Peter K. Lunt, *Mass Consumption and Personal Identity* (Buckingham: Open University Press, 1992)

—— *Talk on Television: The Critical Reception of Audience Discussion Programmes* (London: Routledge, 1994)

Lull, James (ed), *World Families Watch Television* (London: Sage, 1988)

Marc, David, *Demographic Vistas: TV in American Culture* (Philadelphia: University of Pennsylvania Press, 1996)

Marvin, Carolyn, *When Old Technologies Were New* (New York: Oxford University Press, 1988)

Mattelart, Michele and Armand, *The Carnival of the Images: Brazilian Television Fiction* (New York: Bergin & Garvey, 1990)

Macdonald, Gus, *Camera: A Victorian Eyewitness* (London: BT Batsford Ltd, 1979)

MacDonnell, Kevin, *Eadweard Muybridge* (Boston: Little Brown, 1972)

McQuail, Denis, *Mass Communication Theory*, 4th ed (London: Sage, 1994)

McRobbie, Angela, *Postmodernism and Popular Culture* (London: Routledge, 1994)

Mellencamp, Patricia, *Logics of Television: Essays in Cultural Criticism* (Bloomington/London: Indiana University Press/British Film Institute, 1990)

Metz, Christian, *Psychoanalysis and Cinema: The Imaginary Signifier*, trans C. Britton (London: Macmillan, 1982)

Miller, Daniel, *Material Culture and Mass Consumption* (Oxford: Basil Blackwell, 1987)

Millwood Hargrave, Andrea (ed), *The Scheduling Game* (London: John Libbey and Company Ltd, 1995)

Modleski, Tania, *Loving with a Vengeance: Mass Produced Fantasies for Women* (London: Methuen, 1983)

Moores, Shaun, *Interpreting Audiences: The Ethnography of Media Consumption* (London: Sage, 1993)

Morley, David, *Family Television: Cultural Power and Domestic Leisure* (London: Routledge, 1988)

—— *Television, Audiences and Cultural Studies* (London: Routledge, 1992)

Morrison, David, *Television and the Gulf War* (London: John Libbey and Company Ltd, 1992)

Mullan, Bob, *Consuming Television* (Oxford: Basil Blackwell, 1997)

Mulvey, Laura, *Visual and Other Pleasures* (Basingstoke: Macmillan, 1989)

Neale, Steve, *Genre* (London: British Film Institute, 1980)

Neale, Steve and Frank Krutnik, *Popular Film and Television Comedy* (London: Routledge, 1990)

Newcomb, Horace, *Television: The Most Popular Art* (New York:: Anchor Books, 1974)

—— (ed), *An Encyclopaedia of Television*, 3 vols (Chicago and London: Fitzroy Dearborn, 1997)

Nichols, Bill, *Blurred Boundaries* (Bloomington: Indiana University Press, 1994)

Nowell-Smith, Geoffrey (ed), *The Oxford History of World Cinema* (Oxford: Oxford University Press, 1996)

O'Neil, T., *The Game Behind the Game: High Pressure, High Stakes in Television Sports* (New York: Harper & Row, 1989)

Paterson, Richard, 'Planning the family: the art of the television schedule', *Screen Education* 35 (1980), reprinted in M. Alvarado, Edward Buscombe and R. Collins (eds), *Screen Education Reader* (London: Macmillan, 1993)

Powers, R., *Supertube: The Rise of Television Sports* (New York: Conrad-McCann, 1984)

Pratten, Stephen, 'Needs and wants: the case of broadcasting policy', *Media, Culture and Society* 20/3 (July 1998), pp 381-408

Renov, Michael (ed), *Theorising Documentary* (London: Routledge, 1993)

Roberts, J.M., *The Penguin History of Europe* (London: Penguin Books Ltd, 1995)

Scannell, Paddy, *Radio, Television and Modern Life: A Phenomenological Approach* (Oxford: Basil Blackwell, 1996)

Scannell, Paddy and David Cardiff, *A Social History of British Broadcasting 1922-1939* (Oxford: Basil Blackwell, 1991)

Schlesinger, Philip, *Media, State and Nation* (London: Sage, 1991)

Seiter, Ellen, H. Borchers, G. Kreutzner and E. M. Warth (eds), *Remote Control: Television, Audiences and Cultural Power* (London: Routledge, 1989)

Sendall, Bernard, *Independent Television in Britain*, vol 1 (London: Macmillan, 1982)

Shattuc, Joan, *The Talking Cure* (London: Routledge, 1997)

Silj, Alessandro, *East of Dallas: The European Challenge to American Television* (London: British Film Institute, 1988)

Silverstone, Roger, *Television and Everyday Life* (London: Routledge, 1994)

Silverstone, Roger and E. Hirsch (eds), *Consuming Technologies: Media and Information in the Domestic Space* (London: Routledge, 1992)

Smith, Anthony (ed), *Television: An International History* (Oxford: Oxford University Press, 1995)

Sontag, Susan, *On Photography* (London: Penguin, 1978)

Spigel, Lynn, *Make Room for TV: Television and the Family Ideal in Postwar America* (Chicago: University of Chicago Press, 1992)

Stacey, Jackie, *Star Gazing: Hollywood Cinema and Female Spectatorship* (London: Routledge, 1994)

Stratton, John and Ien Ang, 'Sylvania Waters and the spectacular exploding family', *Screen* 35/1 (1994)

Strinati, Dominic and S. Wagg, *Come on Down: Popular Media Culture in Postwar Britain* (London: Routledge, 1992)

Syvertsen, Trine, *Public Television in Transition*, Levender Bilder 5 (Oslo: KULT/NAVE, 1992)

Thompson, Kristin, *Exporting Entertainment: America in the World Film Market 1907-1934* (London: British Film Institute, 1985)

Uricchio, William, *Media, Simultaneity and Convergence: Culture and Technology in an Age of Intermediality*, text of professorial inaugural lecture (Utrecht: Faculteit der Letteren, 1997)

Vahimagi, Tise, *British Television: An Illustrated Guide* (Oxford: Oxford University Press, 1994)

Vaughan, Dai, *Portrait of an Invisible Man* (London: British Film Institute, 1983)

Veljanovski, Cento, *Freedom in Broadcasting* (London: Institute of Economic Affairs, 1989)

Wark, M., *Virtual Geographies: Living With Global Media Events* (Bloomington: Indiana University Press, 1994)

Weis, E. and J. Belton (eds), *Film Sound* (New York: Columbia University Press, 1985)

Whannel, Gary, *Fields in Vision: Television Sport and Cultural Transformation* (London: Routledge, 1992)

Wheen, Francis, *Television* (London: Century, 1985)

White, Mimi, *Tele-Advising* (Chapel Hill: University of North Carolina Press, 1992)

Williams, Raymond, *Television: Technology and Cultural Form* (London: Fontana, 1974)

Wilson, H.H., *Pressure Group: The Campaign for Commercial Television* (London: Secker & Warburg, 1961)

Winston, Brian, *Claiming the Real: The Documentary Film Revisited* (London: British Film Institute, 1995)

—— *Media, Technology and Society: A History from the Telegraph to the Internet* (London: Routledge, 1998)

INDEX